# I Will,
# With God's Help

# I Will, With God's Help

## A Collection of Meditations

### Bo Cox

Forward Movement
Cincinnati, Ohio

Cover design: Amy Svihlik
© 2014, Forward Movement

ISBN 978-0-88028-370-0
Printed in the U.S.A.

**Forward Movement**
www.forwardmovement.org

*This book is dedicated to*

*The Reverend Edward Stone Gleason*

*who was the "help" in*

*"with God's help"*

*for so many, for so long.*

✠

Edward Stone Gleason
July 20, 1933 – October 31, 2013

# Table of Contents

# Foreword

B o Cox was serving a life sentence for murder in the Joseph Harp Correctional Institution in Oklahoma when he won a $3,000 writing prize.

A lifelong reader of *Forward Day by Day* from his early years in Coalgate, Oklahoma, Bo wrote to Charles Long, then editor of Forward Movement, sending a gift of $50 and asking if he might write a month of meditations.

Charles asked Bo to write for November 1995.

When I arrived in Cincinnati in July 1995 to serve as editor, Bo and I were introduced by mail, and I decided to visit him regularly (every six months). This resolve was strengthened when readers' response to Bo's first set of meditations was overwhelming—600 letters, many more than had ever been received by Forward Movement for a single month of meditations. Bo wrote a second time, and we received 900 letters. He continued to write meditations and authored a pamphlet and a book of essays.

Bo has an unusual, uncanny ability to communicate with all kinds of people, especially when he speaks of matters of faith, following Jesus, and welcoming Jesus to become part of one's daily life and walk with God. His language is simple and stark, comes from the heart, and connects with those who want to know the Lord.

My trips to Oklahoma were a highlight of each year. I hated, hated, going into that prison, through two locked doors, but I went to talk with Bo. Sometimes we were locked in the Visitors' Room; at others, we could wander about the prison at will, moving from place to place, greeted by Bo's good friends, many of whom were also murderers.

Forward Movement featured a brief statement about Bo and his photograph in a product catalog. A young woman from Kentucky, who worked in a congregation where the rector was a former student of mine, telephoned to ask for Bo's address. I never gave out such information, but for some reason, I gave her Bo's address. She wrote him, and they corresponded several times; she visited Bo in prison, then moved to Oklahoma to be near Bo. After many prison visits, they fell in love and were married, with Bo in shackles. She devoted herself to achieving Bo's parole and succeeded in June 2003.

What drew me most to Bo was our face-to-face conversation. It was demanding, penetrating, always heartfelt, finally exhausting. I realized this was as close as I would ever come to talking with Jesus in person: the earnestness, the honesty, the clear call to welcome Jesus into my life, hopes, and dreams.

Where does Bo come from? He is a man, born of a woman, who grew through a troubled childhood marked by drug and alcohol addiction and ending with a senseless, violent act when he took the life of another. Then there were years in prison, a life-changing experience through Lifeline (sponsored in part by Episcopal Church Women and The Episcopal Church), a new life dedicated to prayer, discipline, exercise, and writing. How did it all happen? Jesus entered Bo's life, and then Bo succeeded in opening the Way to many others.

— Edward S. Gleason
Editor and Director
Forward Movement
1995-2005

✠

*This foreword was Gleason's last writing for Forward Movement. He died shortly after sending the text, along with a note expressing his joy about this collection.*

# A Note from the Author

My relationship with Forward Movement has spanned almost twenty years. There have been some big changes since November 1995 when my first work appeared. Chief among them is that I am no longer in prison.

However, sitting this morning and gathering my thoughts, it occurs to me that despite the many changes since then, there are more similarities than differences. I am still convinced that God's grace and love is not for sale and can't be earned or deserved. That the power of that love, embodied in Jesus Christ, lies more in his radical walk on earth than it does in his death and the myriad forms of religion based on that death. I still believe that true freedom lies not in the absence of razor-wire fences but in the absence of self. And I still believe more people make bad decisions based in fear than for any other reason.

I still laugh at the irony of my intolerance of people or of belief systems that I find intolerant, and I am easily moved to tears when I open my heart to God's beauty exemplified in all of creation.

Our lives are very much works in progress, and it is in this imperfect state that I once again offer you my writings.

— Bo Cox
2014

✠

# About the Book

This collection of meditations is drawn from the writings of Bo Cox and published by Forward Movement. Because the writings are taken from various publications, you may notice differences in style or length. The excerpts are reprinted in chronological order, although the stories they share may jump around, from childhood memories to incarceration to life today. The sources include:

*Forward Day by Day*: Bo Cox first wrote a month of meditations for *Forward Day by Day* in November 1995. The response was overwhelming. He has since written meditations for *Forward Day by Day* in March and April 1998, March 2001, May, June, and July 2002, April 2011, and February 2014. *Forward Day by Day* is a booklet of daily meditations published by Forward Movement that has provided spiritual sustenance for Christians for more than 75 years.

*Release*: A reprint of the November 1995 set of daily meditations. Republished in 1997.

*God Is Not In the Thesaurus: Stories from an Oklahoma Prison*: This collection of essays was written while Cox was behind bars, serving a sentence for murder. Published in 1999.

*In Transition*: Daily meditations for Lent. Cox wrote these after being released from prison, writing an entry each day and chronicling his early days out of prison. Published in 2004.

*Praying Day by Day, Seeking God Day by Day*: Cox contributed meditations for these publications. These daybooks offer a year's worth of daily reflections. Published in 2009, 2013.

✠

# Introduction

# I Will:
# The Baptismal Covenant

Every time there is a baptism in The Episcopal Church, every baptized person in the congregation joins in renewing his or her own Baptismal Covenant. The covenant begins with statements of belief—the Apostle's Creed in question-and-answer format:

*Celebrant*  Do you believe in God the Father?

*People*  I believe in God, the Father almighty, creator of heaven and earth.

*Celebrant*  Do you believe in Jesus Christ, the Son of God?

*People*  I believe in Jesus Christ, his only Son, our Lord. He was conceived by the power of the Holy Spirit and born of the Virgin Mary. He suffered under Pontius Pilate, was crucified, died, and was buried. He descended to the dead. On the third day he rose again. He ascended into heaven, and is seated at the right hand of the Father. He will come again to judge the living and the dead.

*Celebrant*  Do you believe in God the Holy Spirit?

*People*  I believe in the Holy Spirit, the holy catholic Church, the communion of saints, the forgiveness of sins, the resurrection of the body, and the life everlasting.

The next section is often called the Five Promises of the Baptismal Covenant:

*Celebrant*　　Will you continue in the apostles' teaching and fellowship, in the breaking of bread, and in the prayers?

*People*　　I will, with God's help.

*Celebrant*　　Will you persevere in resisting evil, and, whenever you fall into sin, repent and return to the Lord?

*People*　　I will, with God's help.

*Celebrant*　　Will you proclaim by word and example the Good News of God in Christ?

*People*　　I will, with God's help.

*Celebrant*　　Will you seek and serve Christ in all persons, loving your neighbor as yourself?

*People*　　I will, with God's help.

*Celebrant*　　Will you strive for justice and peace among all people, and respect the dignity of every human being?

*People*　　I will, with God's help.

*The Book of Common Prayer,*
*pp. 304-5*

E ditors at Forward Movement approached Bo Cox with the idea to frame this collection of his writings with the five promises of the Baptismal Covenant. Although Cox embraced the idea as a creative way to share his stories of faith, his first reaction: it might be too "churchy." Indeed, part of the appeal for Forward Movement readers to Cox's writings has been his down-to-earth, often very personal voice, and his honest and sometimes unorthodox musings.

But, as former Forward Movement Editor Edward Gleason wrote in his introduction to *In Transition*, "You and I have come to know Bo Cox, who is a very different person from you and me, but we realize that we have so much in common with him. What we have in common are the central realities of life in Christ that he identifies, describes, makes real in his written words."

The Five Promises of the Baptismal Covenant are precisely about these central realities of life in Christ. They are not doctrinal or churchy. Nor are they clear-cut or straightforward. These promises are guidelines for how we should live out our identity in Christ. Each of us does this differently. Cox's writings reflect one person's intentional and honest engagement in living out his life in Christ. His reflections inspire us to reflect on our own journeys as members of the body of Christ. This is the task of every baptized believer.

As editors sorted through the reflections, it was clear that some fit easily into one promise or another. But many overlapped, incorporating, for example, the teaching component of the first promise and the proclamation aspect of the third. In many ways, this is how life is lived—not in neat boxes that you can check off when complete but rather fluid and integrated. We may understand these promises in different ways—and certainly we live them out in various manners.

The first promise—"Continue in the apostles' teaching and fellowship, the breaking of bread, and in the prayers"—includes formal worship in the church. But it also encompasses all of the ways that we gather with our Christian brothers and sisters, breaking bread and sharing life. It can also include many different forms of prayer. For Bo, this means everything from finding the Divine in nature to the fellowship of recovery meetings to breaking bread together during Holy Eucharist.

The second promise—"Persevere in resisting evil, and, whenever you fall into sin, repent and return to the Lord"—is a lifetime practice for Christians. Evil is always present in the world around us, and it is present in ourselves. This promise names our ongoing need to discern evil and to seek forgiveness from God and from others. It also means we need to forgive ourselves. As a murderer and a recovering alcoholic, Cox constantly wrestles with guilt, repentance, and trusting that he is fully forgiven.

The third promise—"Proclaim by word and example the Good News of God in Christ"—is about much more than simply the words we proclaim. It reflects all we say and all we do. In many ways, these writings are a tangible extension of Cox's proclamation of the Good News of God in Christ. His life was changed when he met Christ in prison, and he continues to proclaim that Good News in his life and writings today.

The fourth promise—"Seek and serve Christ in all persons, loving your neighbor as yourself"—asks us to see Christ in others, even when we find it challenging, or nearly impossible. Loving your neighbor means seeing others as Christ sees them. This is hard enough for all of us in our day-to-day lives. Yet Cox was called to love the prisoner in the neighboring cell, the power-hungry guard, and the family members of his victim. He was sometimes called to love those whom our society despises and fears.

The fifth promise—"Strive for justice and peace among all people, and respect the dignity of every human being"—calls us to look at how we live our public lives. Through his conviction and imprisonment, Cox certainly became familiar with the justice system in our country. Yet, a biblical understanding of justice goes beyond laws and punishment. All of us are called to seek justice and peace for all. This includes respecting the dignity of every human being, even those we find hard to love, or those who have harmed us, or those with whom we disagree. Cox urges us to look at conditions that create environments ripe for bad decisions, and his identity as both teacher and murderer, as faithful Christian and fallen sinner, forces us to look at how we respect the dignity of all people.

For nearly twenty years, Cox has been one of Forward Movement's most popular writers, not only during his imprisonment but also since his release. It's clear that his voice resonates within us, with our own struggles and triumphs in living out the Baptismal Covenant.

The promises of the Baptismal Covenant are made up of active verbs: continue, persevere, proclaim, seek, serve, and strive. Through these stories and reflections, you'll witness an active life of faith. We hope you will find your own convictions and promises strengthened as you read about Cox's journey. And that, like him, in your words and deeds, in your life and love, you will confidently say, "I will, with God's help."

— The Editors,
Forward Movement

# Chapter 1

✠

# Continue

*Will you continue in the apostles'*
*teaching and fellowship,*
*in the breaking of bread,*
*and in the prayers?*

I will, with God's help.

# Keeping the Lamp Lit

*Release: Meditations from Prison, Day 4, 1995*

✠

*Be dressed for action and have your lamps lit;*
*be like those who are waiting for their master*
*to return from the wedding banquet*
*so that they may open the door for him*
*as soon as he comes and knocks.*
— LUKE 12:35-36

"Being" a Christian is a "doing" behavior. It's not something I can simply be. I've got to get off the couch, get dressed for action, and then take action.

In other parts of the gospel, we are told not to hide the light of our lamps to let them shine. In order for my lamp to shine, I've got to keep it lit. How do I do this? Hitting my knees every morning before I do anything else is the first action I take each day. That gets my lamp lit.

There are many ways that I keep my lamp burning. Continuing to listen to God's gentle voice throughout the day and trying to follow his directions are some things I strive to do. Helping, forgiving, loving, and praying for others are other lamplighters. Some days it seems that I never really get a good flame going in my lamp; those are days when I've got to keep asking God for a light.

Jesus told us that he's coming back. Is this a trick? Is our Lord trying to see how many people he can catch off guard? I think not. I believe God is giving us ample time to "light our lamps."

# Come to Supper!

*Release: Meditations from Prison, Day 14, 1995*

✛

*And the angel said to me,*
*"Write this: Blessed are those who are*
*invited to the marriage supper of the Lamb."*
*And he said to me, "These are true words of God."*
— REVELATION 19:9

The book of Revelation has always scared me. Still does. I can't help but focus on all the destruction and death that takes place. When I watch the news I think it is not unlike the chaos described in this apocalyptic prophecy.

There is so much pageantry, so many awesome visions, so many fantastic metaphors in this book that I find myself scratching my head a lot. What, exactly, is the deal?

Is God trying to scare us with the message he sent through John? I don't think so. I think, instead, that God is telling us how, ultimately, good will triumph over evil.

We, the church, are someday going to be wed with Jesus.

We will be invited to the marriage supper of the Lamb. What do we do in the meantime?

I find Holy Communion to be a most adequate appetizer for that final marriage supper with Jesus, the Lamb of God.

Lord, help me listen for your "true words."

# Forward Day by Day

*Friday, March 6, 1998*

✠

*"Why does he eat with tax collectors and sinners?"*
— MARK 2:16B

I was writing a poem, and I'd come to a place where I wanted to use a synonym for God. I highlighted God and moved my cursor to the thesaurus icon at the top of the screen. I clicked.

God is not in the thesaurus, it said.

What? I chuckled at my computer's obvious lack of God-consciousness and began to get this mental image of God being everywhere, even in laptops. I've always thought God was in heaven and maybe in church. But he's also in here, where murderers, thieves, rapists, child molesters, drug dealers, and robbers live. Among society's outcasts, that's where I found God. (Actually, it's where he found me: God wasn't lost. I was.)

You know, it really shouldn't be surprising (but it is, isn't it?) that God could be in a prison. If Jesus were walking around today, what would people think about a son of God who spent most of his time in prisons, visiting the very people society had exiled? In crack houses? Shooting galleries? In parks with the homeless? Juvenile detentions? Mental institutions? Homes for unwed mothers? Slums?

To be Christ-like is to eat with sinners.

Jesus. Have you seen him lately?

Who have you been eating with?

Pass the salt. Thank you.

# Forward Day by Day

✠

*He asked then, "How many loaves do you have?"*
*They said, "Seven."...They ate and were filled;*
*and they took up the broken pieces left over, seven baskets full.*
*Now there were about four thousand people.*
— MARK 8:5, 8-9

Do you have questions? I do.

I think it's a long stretch of the imagination, seven loaves of bread feeding four thousand men. Then again, so was spitting in a deaf man's ear and restoring his hearing. Assuming the little girl was dead and not asleep, so was her miraculous recovery. Exorcising the neighborhood lunatic and placing his demons inside a herd of pigs, then driving them over a cliff...It gets pretty far-fetched.

Just about the time I want to give up on miracles as literal history, I think about all the sighted and hearing people I know who were once blind and deaf, who now see and hear with exhilarating clarity. Many of us were dead in a myriad of ways and are oh-so-much alive today.

Seven loaves. Four thousand satisfied stomachs. Is it a literal transcription of that afternoon, or some sort of symbolic parable? Actually, either way, it works for me. Sometimes I can say I believe and know why, and other times I can say I believe and still have questions.

Bottom line? I believe in miracles. That in itself is a miracle.

I have come to believe that deaths are opportunities for new births. New life after death is what lasts forever and reigns supreme. This has empowered me to live my life in a brand-new way. I am no longer afraid of dying, and he has opened up an eternity of living.

---

I Will: Continue

# Forward Day by Day

✠

*Then he took a loaf of bread,*
*and when he had given thanks,*
*he broke it and gave it to them, saying,*
*"This is my body, which is given for you.*
*Do this in remembrance of me."*
*And he did the same with the cup after supper,*
*saying, "This cup that is poured out for you*
*is the new covenant in my blood."*

— LUKE 22:19-20

As a young acolyte, the shroud of mystery surrounding these words captured my imagination. Father Bill and I would arrange all the sacraments on the little table. I'd count heads so we'd know how many "breads" to put out. I remember feeling a bit priestly myself as I would stand with my towel on my arm, ready to serve.

Our church was an old church, complete with open-face beams in the ceiling and lots of heavy stained glass windows. The result was a mystical, medieval look. Shafts of murky, colored light split the dusk-like atmosphere. I thought Father Bill, with his long hair and beard, looked a lot like what I imagined Jesus would look like. Then, he'd raise the bread and wine above his head into those different hues of inked light. Bathed in the unearthly glow, the chalice and paten were transformed. When Father Bill spoke, you knew it was a holy moment.

I'm more than a little sad that I strayed away from all that. But, at the same time, I'm thankful I made my way back to the altar.

# Forward Day by Day

*Sunday, April 19, 1998 — 2 Easter*

✤

*A week later his disciples were again in the house,*
*and Thomas was with them. Although the doors were shut,*
*Jesus came and stood among them and said, "Peace be with you."*
— JOHN 20:26

I've begun wearing a peace sign around my neck. It's a reminder to me. I can get so overwhelmed with all the complications of Christianity that I forget what it is I'm called to do. That's why the peace sign. It's a simple symbol of what my faith is all about. Peace is just like the cream in milk. If you let it sit, it'll rise to the top. Likewise, peace rises to the top when I let the milk of who and what God is be still and when I quit trying to stir it to my liking.

I can't begin to count the times I've sat in church just not quite getting the spark I needed that day. It wasn't that the sermon was a snoozer. It wasn't that the scripture reading didn't have a ring of truth to it. It wasn't the music. It wasn't the creeds or the collects. It was just that I needed to have Jesus put his arms around me and say, "Peace be with you."

So when it came time for the peace to be passed and I received that first hug and heard another's voice say, "Peace be with you," when I erased another's long face with my own hug and peace, or when I finally smiled at a person I'd been holding a grudge against, well, then I had a more visceral grasp on what it means to be a Christian.

Peace.

# Silent Night

*God Is Not In the Thesaurus:*
*Stories from an Oklahoma Prison, 1999*
*(Also published as a Forward Movement pamphlet in 1996)*

✠

*Then an angel of the Lord stood before them,*
*and the glory of the Lord shone around them,*
*and they were terrified.*
*But the angel said to them,*
*"Do not be afraid; for see—I am bringing you*
*good news of great joy for all the people."*
— LUKE 2:9-10

Christmas. I've got a friend who tells me he dreads this time of year. He gets angry when he hears all those Christmas songs. I don't understand. I wish I could feel the same chills run up my spine when I hear those songs in July as I do when I hear them this time of year. I wish the free-giving spirit that seems to prevail during this season would stay with me year-round, not to mention those blessings that come with being a prolific giver. Above all, I wish it were always this easy to love.

Of course it hasn't always been this way. Once Christmas was pure: the thrill of waking up at three or four in the morning to run into the living room to see if Santa had really eaten all the cookies, the innocent joy as my little brother's face lit up on his first few Christmases. He was so happy in his blissful ignorance of the future. I suppose we all were.

My girlfriend came to our house the Christmas I was in the ninth grade. She was the love of my life, our relationship dating back to the seventh grade. We crept upstairs, where we lay on the floor and kissed. I was the happiest boy in the world that Christmas.

Dad was in rare form too. The last few years I'd noticed a difference in Dad. Something was eating him up and all the whiskey in the world couldn't hide his haunted look as Christmas rolled around. The stranger who'd been visiting these last few years wasn't my dad. But this night was different. Somehow, I think he knew how important it was for me to impress my girlfriend, and he didn't let me down.

After that year, Christmas became hell. Booze, drugs, and a broken family took its toll on me and my Christmas spirit, and it wasn't long before I found a way to deal with life, especially during this emotional and turbulent time of the year. Life, especially the holidays, was a time to party. Staying completely numb was the only way to beat the Christmas blues—and that was how I spent the next twelve years, and all the Christmases too.

In 1990 something changed. In April, after four years in the penitentiary, I'd made a tentative decision to try to get by without getting high. It was relatively easy, mostly because I was tired of the misery that goes along with being out of control of one's life. I was on what recovering alcoholics and addicts call the "pink cloud" stage of recovery—you think now that you've put the chemicals down, life is a bowl of cherries. As happy as I was, the closer it came to Christmas, the more I felt uncomfortable about it. I couldn't put my finger on it, but I knew I was definitely bothered by the impending holiday.

Fortunately, I was around a number of caring people who were also trying to experience a sober Christmas. At first I tried to hide in my cell and not let everyone see the tears welling up every time I'd hear a Christmas song—not only on TV, but for eighteen hours a day on the loudspeakers across the prison compound. I couldn't go anywhere the days before Christmas without crying. I hid it pretty well. By the time Christmas Day actually rolled around, none of my friends knew what was going on inside me. I was scared. There was this enormous amount of emotion building up and ready to burst, and I thought there was something wrong with me.

Christmas night, after hiding in my cell all day, I was persuaded to attend a meeting of alcoholics and addicts. I'd been going to these meetings religiously up until then, but that night I wanted to be alone. I was afraid. I was terrified. The powerful passions boiling inside me were too much. I had to be the only person in the world this scared, and I was embarrassed to let anyone know how much I wanted to cry, how much I felt like a twelve-year-old boy instead of a twenty-seven-year-old man who had spent four years in prison and felt like he had to be tough.

As I sat through the meeting, I continued to suppress the rising wave inside me. I'd look around the room, and as I listened to others talk about how they were handling Christmas without staying loaded and numb, I began to realize this wasn't a bed of roses for anyone. People were telling how they'd been wondering all day what their families were doing on the outside and if they were missed as much as they were missing. I discovered that a lot of us had suppressed the spirit of Christmas during our using and drinking days and were now feeling overwhelmed with the power of that spirit. I wasn't the only one who was afraid!

As the meeting drew to a close, a man named Moses asked if we'd care to join hands, turn off the lights, and sing a song. Hesitantly, the words to "Silent Night" began to fill the dark prison chow hall. In an instant, the song took on a life of its own. It came alive. A bunch of ex-drunks and ex-junkies, thieves, murderers, rapists—society's outcasts—were singing like their lives depended on it. And they did. Suddenly, I felt a presence in the room. Someone, or something, was in the room with us, and it was powerful. Warmth flowed from the top of my head down to the bottom of my feet. As the tears rolled down my cheeks, I knew I'd just met God, and he'd shown me what Christmas was all about. As the song ended and the lights came back on, I looked around the room at all the red eyes and glowing faces, and I knew they knew. I wasn't afraid anymore.

This Christmas, if you're feeling afraid, depressed, or if you just need to know you're not alone, hum a few bars of "Silent Night," and I promise you somewhere in an Oklahoma prison there will be a group of people singing with you. We'll be together in the truest sense of the word.

The angel was right. Don't be afraid. There is great joy coming.

# Is Anybody Out There?

*God Is Not In the Thesaurus:*
*Stories from an Oklahoma Prison, 1999*

✤

*I call aloud upon the Lord;*
*and he answers me from his holy hill.*
— PSALM 3:4

*God is not a cosmic bellboy for whom*
*we can press a button to get things done.*
— HARRY EMERSON FOSDICK

Not long ago I heard a friend exclaim: "I just want God to send me a good woman." And a second man replied, "Send God a Request to Staff."

Most of my prayer life has resembled leafing through a Neiman Marcus Christmas catalog. My prayer life has been a long list of "I wants." When I'm not busy presenting God with a shopping list, I often say, "Okay, God, get me out of this one, and I promise I won't do that again."

From my present vantage point, atop a single bunk bed, looking at four concrete walls, a steel door, and a window with a view of double twelve-foot razor-wire fences designed to keep me here forever, it appears God hasn't heard my last "get me out of this one" prayer. Looking around the cell that Skip and I share, it's pretty obvious God hasn't been to Neiman Marcus either.

My question is: Why bother? It's pretty obvious prayer doesn't work as well as religious folk want to believe. If it did, I'd be home, flopped on the couch. As it is, my home is the state prison, and the only couch I'm likely to see today is this bunk bed.

Prayers. Do they work? All the time? Sometimes? Only certain prayer? What's the deal?

His name is Moses, and his picture is on my wall. Moses used to come here as a volunteer, back in the late '80s and early '90s, and he taught me the meaning of the word "holy." He showed me I could be a sensitive, spiritual person, have a real relationship with my creator, and not be a dogmatic zealot, condemning everyone who failed to believe what I believed. He taught me this and much more. Moses showed me how to walk in love. And he taught me about prayer.

Every time Moses left, we would stop at the front gate, put our arms around each other, bow our heads together in a tight little circle, and pray. We didn't pray for material things; we prayed for spiritual things— love, peace, joy, and faith.

During one of Moses' visits, his wife was in critical condition following surgery. He told us he'd been sitting at the hospital, worrying and praying, afraid to leave, when he felt a need to come to prison. So, he drove out to tell us what was going on and ask for our prayers.

The next week after he gave us the news that his wife had pulled through and was going to be fine, he told us that the week before, on the way home from prison, he had experienced an overwhelming assurance that she was okay. He realized that he had been instructed to leave the hospital and go to our prison. As I sat and listened, I shivered. It wasn't cold.

Moses told us that as a result of the complications she suffered, the doctors said she would never be able to have children. Two years later, Moses again asked for our prayers, this time requesting God's help in having a baby. I thought he was pushing it, but Moses seemed to believe. That helped me to believe.

Again, we prayed. I even asked Moses, joking, what he wanted: a boy or girl?

That picture of Moses on my wall shows him holding Zara, his two-year-old daughter.

Not too long ago a man approached me as I was about to begin exercising. He works out too, so this was not out of the ordinary. We often talked, trading bits of information and advice on the less-than-perfect science of getting in shape. This time something was different.

"Hey, man." I said. "What's up?"

"I've been looking for you."

"What's going on?"

His lip started trembling as he tried to open his mouth and tell me. Nothing came out.

"What's going on brother? What is it?"

"It's my mom," he finally managed to whisper. "She's got a tumor."

He sobbed, and I couldn't do anything but reach out and put my hand on his shoulder.

"I'm sorry," was my weak reply. What could I say?

"I came to ask you to pray for her." He looked straight into my eyes.

Why me? I thought, but the look in his eyes commanded respect, and I said, "Sure. What's her name?"

He told me, dried his eyes, and walked off, leaving me standing there wondering: Why me? I really like him and consider him one of my favorite people, but we are not close friends. We talk when we see each other, but we don't hang out together. We've talked of spiritual matters before, but not often. Why me? It kept going through my thoughts.

That night as I prayed, I asked God to heal his mother and to comfort him and the family. As soon as the words escaped my lips, the neatest thing happened. Let me explain that I'm a bit uncomfortable telling you that God spoke to me, but the minute those prayers left my mouth, I felt, more than I heard, "It's okay."

I knew she was going to be okay. Of course, the doubt set in when I realized that in believing that I'd heard this answer, I was saying God had spoken to me. Would I tell anyone? I couldn't deny the certainty of what I'd experienced, but at the same time, I don't usually tell people God talks to me. Still, I had to tell the guy.

I saw him the next day.

"Guess what? Last night when I prayed, I, well, uh, man, I feel kinda weird saying this, but I swear it's the truth…anyway…last night when I prayed, I got this feeling, but it was more than a feeling, it was, like, well, like God said, 'It's okay.'" And then I went on, "I promise, I wouldn't go around saying this, except, well, that's exactly what happened. I gotta tell ya."

"I believe you." That's all he said.

At this same time, I was waiting for a ruling from the judge who sentenced me. The faith I felt concerning my friend's situation bled over into my own life, and, before I knew it, I was feeling pretty certain that not only had God heard my prayers concerning my release but had the same plans for my future as I did! I knew that God had answered my prayer for my friend. Why not my prayer too?

A week later, as we were starting a softball game. I was on the mound tossing a few warm-up balls when my friend walked toward me.

"It's benign."

"All right, man." We hugged each other.

"Well, I better let you go. You guys are about to start. I just wanted you to know. Thanks."

"Oh no, man, don't thank me. I didn't do anything." I said.

As he walked off, I had a hard time focusing on the plate. I stood still a moment and lowered my head. I was confused. My tears were more for me than they were for him. The night before, I'd found out that the judge had turned me down. Now, I was wondering why God didn't answer my prayer.

"Thanks, God," I whispered, genuinely grateful for my friend and his mom. And yet more than a little sad that, apparently, God hadn't answered my own prayers. Before the notion could materialize, it happened again. Almost as if God knew what my next thought was going to be, I felt, more than I heard, God say, "Be patient."

I'm trying.

# Forward Day by Day

*Sunday, March 4, 2001 — 1 Lent*

✠

*Jesus answered him, "It is written, 'One does not live by bread alone.'"*
— LUKE 4:4

"What are you giving up for Lent?"

How many times have you heard or asked that question? What are we giving up? And why? Are we giving up chocolate? Been there, done that. How about cussing? Failed, miserably, more than once.

Or, instead of giving something up, are we adding a discipline to our routine? Maybe praying every day. Maybe (don't worry; I've failed at this one too) reading the Bible on a daily basis.

Whatever the case, discipline is Lent's theme. If you're anything like me, you've resisted discipline all your life. I still do. I've got this mistaken belief that freedom and discipline are antithetic. I used to think freedom meant being able to do whatever I wanted, whenever I wanted, with no limits and certainly no consequences.

Slowly, I've learned that the more I'm able to allow myself to give in to discipline, the more I'm given freedom. It's helpful that I'm in prison because it allows me to illustrate the manner of freedom I'm speaking of. It's bigger than razor wire, walls, towers, locks, guns, fences, and even attitudes.

Jesus understood this type of freedom on a level I've only glimpsed. So, "What are you giving up for Lent?" Wrong question. "What are you getting for Lent?" That's the question.

I Will: Continue

# Forward Day by Day

✠

*And do not carry a burden out of your houses*
*on the sabbath or do any work,*
*but keep the sabbath day holy,*
*as I commanded your ancestors.*
— JEREMIAH 17:22

Here's a commandment we've got to knock the dust off before we say, "Oh, yeah. I remember that one." What is the big deal, really, about Sundays? After all, isn't work honorable?

Could be that God is telling us that we are more than what we do. We are more than CEOs, administrators, bosses, supervisors, salesmen, or dependable employees. We are more than the number of zeroes in our salary. We are more than the size of our garages, more than how long it takes to mow our front lawn. We are more than x number of years without an absence, more than a guaranteed retirement.

We are more than what we do.

It's funny. I had to come here, where I was a nobody, to learn that.

Even then, I used to think I could maybe work my way out, become somebody, and that would erase the person I was—and I could be someone else.

Then God told me it didn't matter in his eyes what I did. I was still his, and I'd been so all along.

I don't know if I could spend a day every week basking in that unfathomable gift.

But I know he wants me to try. Because, after all, I could do that for the rest of my life and still not understand…I am more than what I do.

# Forward Day by Day

*Friday, May 24, 2002*

✠

*Do not receive into the house*
*or welcome anyone who comes to you*
*and does not bring this teaching.*
— 2 JOHN 10

Some of my Christian literalist friends and I get into arguments about the Bible. Frequently. To me, the Bible is confusing. As far as I'm concerned, that's not a bad thing to say. In fact, it comes closer to loving my God with all my heart, mind, and soul than confessing that I believe something I don't understand or don't agree with—mainly because it's the most honest statement I'm capable of making.

When I say this to my strict friends, they claim that if one word of the Bible is not true then none of it is true, and they might as well throw it away. But they really don't want to throw it away because they're very sure of what they know.

When I was a child, I had a friend whose parents were wealthy. Every time a new toy came out, he had it. It was fun playing with him and all those new toys. Thing was, in the self-centered surety that came with his parents meeting all of his materialist needs, he was very sure of the rules of his sandbox. When I would challenge his authority, he would invariably threaten to take his toys and go in the house.

Now people want to do that with the Bible. When Jesus said for us to become like children, I don't think that's what he meant.

# Forward Day by Day

*Wednesday, May 29, 2002*

✛

*Without any doubt,*
*the mystery of our religion is great.*
— 1 TIMOTHY 3:16A

This seemingly simple admission was right on time this morning. You see, it's been a bit scary this time around, writing these meditations. I've been struggling. The words haven't come easy. Maybe it's a case of writer's block. Or, maybe it's that the more I try, the more I see how ill-equipped I am to describe the Alpha and the Omega.

It's like I've been commissioned to color a picture. God hands me one of those jumbo-size box of crayons and says, "Here. Color this. I'm a sunrise." So I get out my oranges, purples, and reds. Just when I think I'm done, God says, "I'm also night."

The next day my assignment is a clear blue sky. I like the way crayons are arranged in progressive shades. I use every hue of blue there is, and I think I've done a magnificent job of capturing God as the sky. Then God says, "I'm going to cloud up and rain."

Next time, it's a tree, and I'm starting to catch on so I ask, "Is it summer or winter?" and God laughs at me and says, "Fall."

I've got an admission to make. I'm not a very good artist. I feel like I'm running out of crayons while there are still so many pictures to go. Not only that, I think I've colored outside the lines on more than a few of my pictures.

Then God says, "Color me human."

# Forward Day by Day

*Monday, July 1, 2002 — Canada Day*

✛

*Whatever you ask for in prayer with faith,*
*you will receive.*
— MATTHEW 21:22

Two weeks ago, I was granted the first stage of parole. I've still got a ways to go before I walk out the door. In fact, there are at least two more phases between me and physical freedom. I've still got to pass stage two and get the governor's signature before the prison experience is over.

During my drug-using years, I didn't pray. Fifteen years ago, when I was in the county jail awaiting trial, I begged God to get me out of this. The above scripture was shown to me as a guarantee of answered prayer. When I was found guilty and sentenced to life, I told God, "Thanks a lot, for nothing," and went back to drugs and not praying. Some years later, I sobered up and tentatively stuck my toe in the water again.

This time, I tried not to base my relationship with God on what I could get out of it. I tried not to even pray for myself, except when to do so would enable me to help someone else. As I grew in my walk with the Creator, I began to trust that God loves me more than I can ever imagine and I also grew to understand that, no matter what, in God's world, everything is okay. Oftentimes I don't ask for anything—for me or for anyone else—trusting that the One who made everything doesn't need me as a backseat driver.

Still, a few days before this last parole hearing, I asked God for help.

# In Transition

*Monday, March 8, 2004*

✠

*But he said to them, "I have food to eat that you do not know about."*
— John 4:32

I had not been out of prison a few hours when it hit me: This scary and overwhelming feeling that seemed to say, "You are never going to get what you want." It was a split-second of near panic where I stood eye-to-eye with the stark reality that something was missing and the void could not be filled, at least not with anything I could pick up with my hands, see with my eyes, hear with my ears, taste, or smell. Not with anything outside of me. Not with stuff. Not even with finally being out of prison.

That was it. Being out of prison was not enough. Nothing had changed, I realized as I stood on that sidewalk. I had only been out a few hours, after seventeen years—years in which I had dreamt of this moment as being the most satisfying ever, of wondering if I would ever set foot outside prison again.

There were moments in prison when I realized that my peace, my freedom, my joy, my being was not contingent on where my sneakers stood—and they had been extreme moments of clarity. These were moments when I realized that the Creator of all that is and all that ever will be was beyond all our understanding. I came to understand there was nothing life could throw at me or I could walk into that could define me. But up until this moment on the sidewalk this had all been, in part, a theoretical supposition.

Most of the reason I had embraced such a path was definitely not due to any redeeming qualities on my behalf; it was more a case of survival.

I did not burst onto the scene wanting to practice honesty and tolerance in all my affairs. Heavens, no!

I was in prison, and I was afraid I would die there. That was the impetus for trying this new way.

That desperation and lack of pretense certainly added to the genuineness of my experience, and when I say I had found freedom in a place normally thought to be devoid of such, I mean it with every fiber of my being.

But then they let me out, and it was in that state of conventional freedom that I really began to understand how right I had been. Much in the same manner as my freedom had not been defined by walls and guns and laws, it was not defined by the lack of these either.

There is a hole in me that can only be fed by the food Jesus is talking about in this scripture. The price of this wisdom has been great—at least for me—and I went a long way to learn it. But the cost and the journey add to the meal. I am honored to share it with you.

# In Transition

*Saturday, March 20, 2004*

✛

*You sweep us away like a dream;*
*we fade away suddenly like grass.*
*In the morning it is green and flourishes;*
*in the evening it is dried up and withered.*
— PSALM 90:5-6

The Psalmist is talking about human years being insignificant in light of the infinitude of the Creator. And they are. We are. I had forgotten how much so until I walked out into my backyard sometime during my first week out of prison and looked up at the summer sky and all those stars.

It had been seventeen years since I had seen the stars in their entire splendor. In prison, the halogen lights are so bright, they block the light of all the stars, save for a dozen or so of the brightest. I had completely lost all memory of what it was like to look up and not be able to count them all.

As I stood looking up, I thought of how inconsequential I am. I am merely one of billions of humans who have lived their quick-as-a-wink existences out under the lights of these very same stars, stars that have been around for longer than I can comprehend. These stars were in the same sky Jesus raised his face to.

My first morning out, I went for a run. Running had become a regular part of my life in prison, and I had logged countless miles on the same track for thirteen years. When I stop and think about it, it is almost as mind-boggling as the stars to try and put a number on how many laps I ran in those years. Regardless, it was the same scene repeated approximately every four minutes and fifteen seconds. So when I took off that first day and ran underneath oak trees and in between soy fields, cow pastures, windmills, and barns, it was emotional. When rabbits and squirrels and mockingbirds added their presence to the waving wheat, it was almost too much. Finally, back in my yard, I sat down in a heap and contemplated a yellow dandelion.

In this state of heightened awareness, it occurred to me that I couldn't even cause a dandelion to grow. Sure, I could buy dandelion seeds and fertilizer and even the best potting soil. I can get water and even if the sun won't come out, I could use artificial light. Still, as far as what takes place inside a dandelion goes, as far as the creation of life goes, I am unable to duplicate what I so easily overlook and take for granted everyday.

Sitting cross-legged in the grass, staring at a dandelion, I was as aware of God as I have ever been. Same thing the night before with the stars.

Now that I have been out a few months and am getting into the grind of "normal" life, I find myself worrying about rent, savings, retirement, vacation days, car payments, and other distractions. As I chase this "normal" life, I lose sight of the lesson of the dandelion and the stars.

According to the Psalmist, so did they. That is reassuring and even more indicative of the fact that I am not alone.

Neither are you.

# In Transition

*Sunday, April 4, 2004 — Palm Sunday*

✥

*Ascribe to the LORD the glory due his Name;
worship the LORD in the beauty of holiness.*
— PSALM 29:2

A few weeks earlier, my wife and I attended our very first Eucharist together. I had been attending Eucharist on a semiregular basis for a number of years, thanks to a very committed and good man, Deacon George Day. He's the prison ministry coordinator for the Diocese of Oklahoma and has fed me with the spiritual food of that most precious Body and Blood on more than one occasion. Every time I received communion from George, I felt like I was in the presence of God. You see, George has every reason in the world to hate me and others like me. Yet, week after week, there he was with those kind eyes, feeding me Life itself.

As Debb and I walked into the magnificent old church, I wondered: how could this possibly top what I had been experiencing for the past ten years? Suddenly, the service started: "Blessed be God: Father, Son, and Holy Spirit." That in itself wasn't earth-shattering. It was the priest saying the same words George had said to start all our services in prison.

"And blessed be his kingdom, now and for ever. Amen."

What I wasn't ready for was the response from the people. I had been listening to ten or twenty people say it, most half-heartedly, for the past decade. I had forgotten what a whole church full of people sounded like. My heart leapt up into my throat, and I had to swallow hard not to lose it right there.

The service continued, and I regained my composure. That is, until the choir sang the Gloria. I've never heard angels sing but I think they might sound something like the singing I heard that morning.

You know me; I'm as unorthodox as they come. But I've got to tell you, when they sang, "Lord God, Lamb of God, you take away the sin of the world," I felt like I had been washed clean, and I was left with my head hanging and tears streaming down my face. It's not like I didn't know I was forgiven, but I experienced it on a whole new level that morning. (And, as I find it is with forgiveness, I continue to this day to experience it over and over.)

When I went to take Holy Communion, I looked up from my knees as the celebrant approached and it was none other than another good and faithful prison volunteer who had spent many hours, for as long as I could remember, in prison feeding those of us so in need of being fed. Now, here she was, offering me my very first Eucharist outside of prison. It was too much. I took it with trembling lips and a humbled-to-the-point-of-embarrassed heart.

Over the last few weeks, I may have given you the impression that I don't have anything good to say. In fact, you may think me on the verge of being disillusioned with the whole deal. If you could have seen me that morning, you know how far from the truth that is. In fact, if you could see me right now, you would know.

# Everyone Has a Prison

*Praying Day by Day, 2009*

✠

*We who lived in concentration camps can remember*
*the men who walked through the huts comforting others,*
*giving away their last piece of bread.*
*They may have been few in number,*
*but they offer sufficient proof that everything*
*can be taken from a man but one thing:*
*the last of the human freedoms—*
*to choose one's attitude*
*in any given set of circumstances,*
*to choose one's own way.*
—VIKTOR FRANKL

I was thinking that getting used to being out of prison was perhaps the hardest thing I'd ever done until one day it dawned on me that getting used to being in prison was no cakewalk. I had grown accustomed to prison. Never mind that it was something that at one point in my life would have been unimaginable. Never mind that prison was painful and real and scary. Never mind that it was one of the most traumatic events in a string of traumatic events in my early twenties.

I became so used to prison that when I was released I had difficulty adjusting. At times, I might even have found the familiarity of prison preferable to the unfamiliarity of the outside world. Both then and now, I have more peace when I'm helping others.

Prisons come in myriad forms, and I can tell you three things:

(1) Everyone has a prison.

(2) We can get used to our prisons and think they're the norm, so much so that when we step out, we want back in.

(3) In or out, solace comes by finding and helping others who have more troubles than we do.

If you are standing at the gate of your prison—little matter if you are going in or coming out—trembling at the unknown, take a deep breath and look for someone to help.

# Simple Lessons

*Praying Day by Day, 2009*

✠

*Truly I tell you, unless you change
and become like children,
you will never enter the kingdom of heaven.*
— MATTHEW 18:3

I like to take people from the treatment center where I work to a local park where we go on a recovery walk. Their instructions are to find something in nature (no pulling up live plants!) that represents where they are in their new journey.

Later, as we sit in a circle around an old fire ring, I am amazed at the insights. Having turned away from alcohol and other drugs (including nicotine) for almost two decades, I sometimes fall prey to the misconception that more is better when it comes to sobriety.

But in this circle, where people are just days away from their last binge, I am reminded that all our journeys are day-by-day exercises and their depth is measured by more than years.

In this circle, I am told that a dead piece of wood with moss growing on it is reflective of life in the midst of death; that a smooth rock and rough rock in a trembling palm can remind the holder that even the hardest can change; that a simple forked limb can illustrate the choice we have to be happy or not; and that an acorn in the hand is as valuable as the century-old oak we sit next to because of its potential.

Finally, I am reminded that the same elements that make up the lessons in the circle, the same elements that make the woods and our world, are also the elements we're made of. When I recall that my intent was to teach them something, I have to smile at my arrogance.

# Forward Day by Day

*Sunday, April 3, 2011 — 4 Lent*

✠

*One thing I do know,*
*that though I was blind,*
*now I see.*
— JOHN 9:25B

Reading scripture, meditating on it, maybe even testing it, and then writing about it is beneficial to me. I hope it is equally helpful to you. The process is illuminating and sometimes, ironically, blinding again at the same time. From blindness to sight to a clarity that is blinding at times. What a trip.

One could see my life as a great life. Most of the time, I do—fantastic partner, wonderful parents, loving family, steady job, beautiful home, and two dogs and five cats that are absolutely the best on the planet. All this for a guy who literally had nothing, not even his physical freedom, twenty years ago.

And yet, that is not enough to enable me to see clearly. No more than prison bars could dull my spirit's vision can the material comforts of modern life make it clear.

Sometimes I forget this and begin to think that things and situations can make me happy. I scratch my head, puzzled and upset at myself for walking around angry at nothing in particular and wondering where that hole in my gut comes from and what will make it go away.

And then I remember, and that in itself is blinding. But maybe it's the tears.

# Forward Day by Day

*Wednesday, February 12, 2014*

✠

*For by the grace given to me I say to everyone among you
not to think of yourself more highly
than you ought to think,
but to think with sober judgment,
each according to the measure of faith
that God has assigned.*

— Romans 12:3

I'm not much, but I'm all I think about.

So many decisions each day and most, if not all, of them are centered around self. Each of us has a set of scales—many sets in fact—constantly weighing the pros and cons of every behavior. How will this help? How will this hurt?

A certain degree of this is helpful. For instance, it is wise to not walk across a busy street without looking. However, the instinct to protect self can run amok. Suddenly, protection of self becomes promotion of self. Erroneously, we fear no one else is going to speak up for us, so if we want to be heard or recognized, we better blow our own horn. Either that or, deep down, the way we see ourselves is so distorted that we seek to bolster our perception with self-service.

Seeing ourselves as right-sized can be a lifetime process for some. Finally settling in, we find it fits like nothing else.

# Forward Day by Day

✠

*If we live, we live to the Lord,*
*and if we die, we die to the Lord;*
*so then, whether we live or whether we die,*
*we are the Lord's.*
— ROMANS 14:8

I called my dad a few nights ago, and he'd just returned from visiting a friend who had been stricken with a swift and vicious form of stomach cancer. His friend had already lost much weight and was in constant pain. He and his family had been to some of the best treatment centers in the country and had tried everything.

Finally, they'd gone to a particular doctor and asked for it straight: What would the doctor advise if this were his family member or himself? He told them he wouldn't get the next procedure, and he'd do everything he had ever wanted to do because he wasn't going to be around for very long.

My dad's friend didn't have much of a bucket list; he'd already done more than most of us ever dream of. He told dad he would like to see the spring calf crop come in if he could, but that, all in all, he had his house in order and was ready.

I remember thinking, what a wonderful example of faith—both in life and in dying.

# CHAPTER 2

# Persevere

*Will you persevere in resisting evil,
and, whenever you fall into sin,
repent and return to the Lord?*

I will, with God's help.

# Another Way

*Release: Meditations from Prison, Day 2, 1995*

⊹

*Do not try to prove your strength by wine-drinking,*
*for wine has destroyed many...*
*it has been created to make people happy...*
*Wine drunk to excess leads to bitterness of spirit,*
*to quarrels and stumbling.*
— *ECCLESIASTICUS 31:25, 27, 29

This passage tells us that wine was created to make people happy. Ben Sira, the author, also speaks of the out-of-control whirlwind of addiction that has governed my life and the lives of thousands of others. If your life has been affected by drugs, you'll be happy to know that there is another way to be happy. God has more happiness-capacity than any mind-altering substance.

I'm serving time because, in 1986, after a day and night of drinking, I got into a fight with, and accidentally killed, another young man who was drunk. I know how wine can lead to quarrels and, ultimately, destroy. Before writing this, I prayed hard about whether to disclose this. I was scared people would shut me out. Please don't.

Current statistics tell us that almost 90 percent of the people who are locked up in U.S. prisons are there as a result of drugs and alcohol. I don't need a government study to tell me this. I live here. Ben Sira was telling people the same thing thousands of years ago. God's Word doesn't change. He is the same yesterday, today, and tomorrow.

*From the Apocrypha

# Out of Hell

*Release: Meditations from Prison, Day 20, 1995*

✛

*Besides all this, between you and us a great chasm has been fixed,*
*so that those who might want to pass from here to you cannot do so,*
*and no one can cross from there to us.*
— LUKE 16:26

Luke's description of hell, and finality of it, scares me. It also reminds
me of prison. The great chasm in my case is a double razor-wired
fence, complete with electric sensors, cameras, guards, and bullets.
Because of where my heart was in relation to God, I am here. In Luke's
story, because of where the rich man's heart was in relation to God when
he died, he was in hell.

I'm fortunate. God can and does transcend these fences.

I don't want to believe in God because I'm afraid of going to hell. I
want to believe in him because it is the right and the good thing to do. I
am able to receive so much more when I go to God with a joyous heart.
When I go with a fear-based, foot-dragging attitude, I miss out on the
fact that it is something I get to do, not something I have to do.

A friend once told me, "Religion is for people who are afraid of hell.
Spirituality is for those who have been there."

I guess I'm spiritual.

# Forward Day by Day

✛

*There is nothing outside a person that by going in can defile,*
*but the things that come out are what defile.*
— MARK 7:15

She made me do it. He started it. It's her fault. If he wouldn't have done that, I wouldn't have done what I did.

Have you ever heard yourself say any of the above? I sure have. Accepting responsibility for my behavior has been a problem of mine since early adolescence.

In truth, no one makes me do anything. Hitting someone back, calling someone a name after he called me one, resenting someone after she hurt me, talking about someone behind his back because he was different or any of a thousand other justified behaviors—every single thing I ever did that I thought was a result of an external condition was, in truth, an internal choice on my part.

When you come to prison, they tell you that if someone hits you, you've got to fight back. You don't have a choice. If you don't, they'll be on you like vultures, devouring you because you're weak. I've been in one fight since I've been in. It took place during a basketball game. We exchanged words. The guy hit me. I thought about what everyone believed. I had to do it. No choice. He started it. So, I walked off.

Ultimately, everything I do comes from within.

# Forward Day by Day

*Monday in Holy Week, April 6, 1997*

✠

*A bruised reed he will not break,*
*and a dimly burning wick he will not quench…*
*to open the eyes that are blind,*
*to bring out the prisoners from the dungeon,*
*from the prison those who sit in darkness.*
— ISAIAH 42:3, 7

It was April 6, 1990. The man sitting with his hung-down head in his hands was at the end of his rope. He was a bruised reed, and if his wick was dimly burning, he didn't know it. He was blind to 90 percent of what we know as life. He was prisoner #150656 in a state prison, and yet its towers, razor wire, guns, and locks were hardly comparable to his other prison—the prison within himself. He was sitting in a dark cell, A2-120, and that cell was nothing compared to the dungeon from which he could never escape; its darkness seemed as daylight next to the midnight of his tired, worn out, blackened soul.

"Help." It was a barely perceptible squeak. But, it was all that was needed.

This season is crucial to understanding hope and faith. This week is called Holy Week. The hope contained therein is indeed holy. The faith lies in our ability to believe that this resurrection thing will happen over and over every time we meet a death.

The prisoner? I'm writing this on April 6, 1997. Today is my sobriety birthday. You knew it all along, didn't you?

See? You do believe. So do I.

I Will: Persevere

# Forward Day by Day

*Sunday, April 26, 1998 — 3 Easter*

✠

*He fell to the ground and heard a voice saying to him,*
*"Saul, Saul, why do you persecute me?"*
— ACTS 9:4

Saul wasn't going to the supermarket. He was going to Damascus for the specific purpose of finding people who believed in Jesus and taking them to prison or even killing them. It wasn't his first time; he'd built quite a reputation as a Christian killer. I find it more than significant that the Lord didn't just strike him down there on the Damascus road. After all, he was out to kill good people, people who followed the Lord's son, Jesus. It was a war. Meet might with might, right? Wrong.

He didn't even yell at him. You can almost hear the pleading tone. God has all the power in the world. He is power. And, yet, he's asking Saul, begging him, almost. Yes, the best-known part of the story and the one everyone considers so important is Saul's conversion, and it is important. Anyone who's ever been a "far worse sinner," like myself, has to appreciate Saul/Paul. But notice how God did it.

He didn't kill him, berate him with guilt, or strike him with lightning. As a matter of fact, I get the feeling God wasn't even mad at him. God converted him. Jesus got him on his side. That's so indicative of Love, and it gives me hope that I, too, can be loved back into shape.

If I can, we all can.

# The Old People

*God Is Not In the Thesaurus:*
*Stories from an Oklahoma Prison, 1999*

✥

*Whoever welcomes one such child in my name welcomes me,*
*and whoever welcomes me welcomes not me but the one who sent me.*
— MARK 9:37

St. Peter's Episcopal Church smelled like mothballs. I hated it.

Only old people went there. It was like sitting in a retirement home. Besides, I couldn't understand that weird, archaic language. Why did we always have to read the same boring stuff from the same book? The monotony and rote were worse than school.

To make matters worse, across the street was the Baptist Church where the majority of my schoolmates attended. Over there, it seemed, there weren't any adults and no old people. On their huge front lawn, amid screams of joy and much laughter, hordes of young people played—are you ready for this?—games. That's right. While my senses were being subjected to hard oak pews, dim lights, foreign language, and an overwhelming smell of Absorbine Jr., stale cigarette smoke, Sweet Garrett snuff, and mothballs, my schoolmates were playing volleyball, softball, and tag. God appeared to be a lot more fun on the other side of the street, and, as a young boy, I wondered why I couldn't have been born a Baptist.

During my early teenage years, church got better. We got a new priest, Father Bill Winston; let me call him Bill. He had long hair and a beard, and in my first theological reflection, I wondered if Jesus looked like Father Bill. Not only did Bill represent a kinder, gentler God, he involved me in the services. When I became an acolyte, what we did in the Episcopal Church began to take on a whole new meaning. Bill's teachings started to shine much-needed light on the confusing services and before long I began to appreciate what was going on and developed relationships with older people. Things that had made no sense, like the mysticism of Communion and the symbolism of candlelight, became captivating.

But not as captivating as drugs. The flicker of church candles on the shadowed altar faded in the glow of burning marijuana in the back seats of cars on dark country roads. A sip of wine at Communion with my Lord was lost in endless gulps of liquor and oblivion from life and from my Lord. The seasoned counsel of elders, who loved me enough to tell me the truth even when I didn't want to hear it, gave way to the counsel of well-intentioned, unaware peers, whose best advice was to try anything once, and if it felt good, do it again. I took things a step further, and if it felt good, I overdid it.

Before I began to quit everything else, I quit church. Later I quit basketball. (The coach had it in for me.) I quit college. (I wasn't cut out for it. Everyone was fake.) I quit every job. (Some unreasonable boss would invariably fire me for no reason.) I even quit obeying laws. (They were unfair.)

The only thing I wouldn't quit was getting high and drinking. This was my new religion. In the forgetfulness of chemicals, I found the only peace I knew: peace from myself and from the consequences of the way I was living. It wasn't too long before my marijuana and alcohol habit turned into an anything-that-would-get-me-away-from-the-reality-of-life habit.

I was in that altered, yet familiar, state the night I killed Bart.

Four months later, I was on my way to prison with a life sentence.

I remember the day they brought me to prison. Coming from a small town meant you knew everyone, and everyone knew you. The deputy sheriff who took me to prison was a guy who'd been a few years ahead of me in high school. I knew him and his whole family, and he knew me and mine. Although I'd already been in solitary confinement in the county jail for four months, I still had no idea what to expect. Any given day in our small county jail resembled an episode from *The Andy Griffith Show*. That is why, when we pulled up to the huge, ominous building surrounded by the double, twelve-foot fences topped with razor wire, complete with armed guards at the gate, I got scared. I wanted to reach out and hug the deputy and beg him not to make me get out.

But I didn't. I played it tough. I smiled and joked and acted like I wasn't scared. Looking back, I'm sure that my little act was transparent. We pulled through the big double gates, and I got out, went inside the electronic doors into a new world. Bill took my chains off, told me to take care of myself, turned, and left.

"What's your name?" the guard asked without looking at me, although I was looking at him, trying to catch his eye to let him see I was a nice person.

"Bo Cox." I replied.

"I don't need a first name, Cox. Your number is one-five-oh, six-five-six. Remember it."

Another guard came up. "Move along to the next door. Wait until they call your number. Step inside. No talking. Don't cross the yellow line. Move it."

I tried to smile at him to show him that I would try to get along, but there was no use. He wasn't having any of it, and suddenly I was beginning to get a taste of what my life was going to be like.

Over the next four hours I was stripped, had every orifice in my body probed, my head shaved, my clothes replaced with an orange jumpsuit, was yelled at, crammed into starkly lit, closet-sized rooms with other jumpsuited men, and herded around like cattle until that night, when they finally put me in my own cell. I was in prison.

Another stern-faced guard showed me to my cell, unlocked the door, and stepped aside as I walked in. Lying on the bottom of two steel bunks attached to the wall was a man wearing coveralls like mine, the top rolled down around his waist, his torso covered by tattoos. He was reading a paperback. At his side, on the edge of an empty cardboard-box-turned-coffee-table, sat a stained Styrofoam cup full of coffee and a dented Pepsi can with a hand-rolled cigarette sitting on top, trailing smoke to the ceiling. Even though this was a new world, something told me none of this was new to my cellmate. He seemed completely at home.

"Hey, what's up?" he said, as the guard locked the door behind me.

"Hi. How ya doin'?" I nodded. I put my belongings—one thin plastic mattress, a set of dirty-white sheets, one yellowed towel, a plastic covered pillow, a small plastic bag containing my toothpaste, shampoo, and soap, and three pairs each of grungy gray boxers, socks, and shirts—up on the top bunk—and sat down.

"You smoke?" he offered me one.

"Thanks man, I got one," I said and pulled out my cigarettes. I'd already heard about accepting "free" gifts from other prisoners.

"First time in?"

"Yeah."

"What for?"

"First-degree murder."

"C'mon, man. Really. You ain't gotta lie. What is it? Drugs? Hot checks?"

"Na, I'm serious, man. First-degree murder."

"I can't believe it," he said. "Look at you. First-degree murder. Uh-uh, I ain't believin' it. You look like some college kid, 'cept for that shaved head."

He laughed at his little joke, and I managed a smile even though nothing was funny.

We talked. He told me about doing time. What to do. What not to do. As we talked into the night, I found myself feeling a little more comfortable with the place where I was destined to exist. Still, I just didn't want to believe this was happening. I remember going to sleep that first night, praying that when I woke up this would all be a dream.

When I awoke, it was all very real, and, although nothing miraculous had happened during the night to make the nightmare disappear, I did make a huge discovery.

There were drugs here. Before lunch of my second day in prison, I had found some weed, bought it with some of the cigarettes I had, and got high. As the potent marijuana began to soothe me, I decided that as long as I could get high, I could do prison. I still wanted out, but over the course of the next few years, the drugs worked their magic, and I eventually lost sight of that. All I wanted was to be high. Oh, sure, if you asked me, I'd tell you I wanted out, but in reality I wanted to be high. It got to a point where it didn't matter what it was: weed, homemade beer, crank, heroin, coke, or anything injectable. I even tried paint thinner and drank the alcohol squeezed out of bars of Right Guard deodorant because I wanted to be high. Nothing more. Certainly nothing less.

I'd been living like that for eleven years, four of them in prison, when it finally quit working for me.

There were many factors, but I was acutely aware of three reasons that I needed to lay the chemicals down. I woke up one morning, and, seemingly in an instant, it was clear that I was spiritually dead. There was nothing left inside. I just couldn't get high enough anymore to ignore that or the tragic shape of my life. What is more, I realized that as long as I continued to get high I had zero chance of getting out of prison.

I had to try to quit getting high. So I did. Tried. That's all it was at first: a wobbly, fearful step into the scary world of reality.

I remember back in the late '70s and early '80s, when my drug use had just begun, there was a saying: "Drugs are for people who can't handle reality." The counterculture came up with an answer to that: "Reality is for people who can't handle drugs." The truth was, in the beginning days of my sobriety, I didn't know if I could handle either.

Somehow I made it. A week passed. I didn't get high. Then, two weeks; then, a month. Almost before I knew it, I had ninety days under my belt. Ninety days without getting high. I couldn't believe it. All my friends were freaking out. They couldn't understand why. Some of them became paranoid around me, thinking I was going "straight." I'll never forget one old-time convict and dope fiend who cussed me out, saying that I'd "sold out to the man." And, in a way, I felt like I had. My whole identity had been wrapped up in the getting, selling, and using of drugs. Without that, I was naked. I was a nobody.

For the first couple of months, the only thing I changed was my using. I simply did what recovering alcoholics and addicts call "white-knuckling"—didn't get high. Everything else was the same. All my friends still used. I still hung out in the cell when everyone else was getting high. I would still buy and re-sell drugs for a small profit. I was still in the mix and something told me that if I didn't change that, it wouldn't be long until I was right back where I had started.

Not coincidentally, there happened to be an alcohol and drug treatment program at my prison, and there were people I knew in that program who were actually clean and sober. I knew, beyond question, I needed to get in that program, but there was a nine-month waiting list. I couldn't wait for nine months, and if I started getting high again, I was afraid I'd not be able to stop.

I went and spoke with the director of the program who told me I was accepted, but it would be close to a year before I'd be able to move to the housing unit where the program was located. I remember telling him that I'd been clean for about three months. Was there any way to move me up on the list? He shook his head and told me he was sorry.

I walked out of his office in a state of desperation. What was I going to do?

Before I got back to my cell, I had an idea.

I knew that the drug program was funded, in part, by The Episcopal Church. Even though I'd turned my back on church, God, and the people of St. Peter's, I wondered if there was a chance they'd help get me accelerated admission into the program. The more I thought about it, the more it seemed plausible. At the very least, it couldn't hurt to ask. All they could do was tell me, "No, you had your chance."

I wrote a letter to St. Peter's in Coalgate, saying that I had a drug problem, I needed and wanted help, and it was going to take too long, in my opinion, for me to get that help. I didn't feel that I deserved help, and I was afraid. My plea was simple: If there is anything, anything at all, that you could do to help me, I need it.

I mailed the letter and told myself I'd give it at least two more weeks. I didn't expect anything. After all, they were just a poor, small parish in the southeast corner of our state. And who was to say they wouldn't decide I'd had my chance? It certainly wasn't their fault I was where I was.

A week later, I got a letter from the senior warden at St. Peter's.

"Dear Bo," it began. "Enclosed, you'll find a copy of the letter we sent to the bishop. We hope it helps. You're in our prayers."

I opened the copy of the letter they'd sent to the bishop and began reading. Tears welled in my eyes. They told him about the boy they remembered, the young acolyte with the bright eyes and ready smile. The young man with potential. Me. They told him how I'd left church, and how tragic the following years were, not only to me, but to those who loved me. And, most endearing to me, they told him that what had happened four years ago was a terrible, terrible thing, but, nonetheless, an accident.

That was my first experience with forgiveness. They finished up the letter by telling the bishop they wanted this young man back and implored him to intervene and, please, help me get into the treatment program.

Later that same day, I was called back to the director's office. He looked at me with raised eyebrows, a mildly suspicious smirk on his face. "I don't know what you did," he said. "But whatever it was, it worked."

I began to smile.

"Go back to your unit and pack your stuff. You're moving to the Lifeline Program this afternoon."

The young acolyte isn't young anymore. He's been in a medium-security prison since July 26, 1986. He hasn't picked up a drink or any other drug since April 6, 1990. Somewhere along the way he began a relationship with God. His eyes are once again bright; he's gotten his smile back, and he often dreams of the day he can go back and take Communion with the people who saved his life.

# Forward Day by Day

*Thursday, March 1, 2001*

✠

*For you are a people holy to the LORD your God.*
— DEUTERONOMY 7:6A

"Why do prisoners always get religion once they land in jail?" It's a fair enough question.

Stop and consider what it must feel like, that first morning you wake up and realize that you've burnt every bridge you ever had. You've come to a point where drugs—and that's if you can get them—won't even dim your severe reality. There is literally nowhere to turn. So in desperation, not because you're a good person or looking to serve God, you ask, "Help. Please."

To tell the truth, you don't really expect anything. Even though you might not have attended regularly, you paid attention in church when you were a kid and you still think God prefers good people over bad. Still. This is the only place left. The last chance. Why not try before giving up?

Whether this is your first time reading these words from prison or your third, I pray that you know this: You and I are no different. I know you need him as much as I do. Regardless who asks, the next time you hear the question, "Why do prisoners always get religion once they land in jail?" you can say, "Maybe it's the only way left when you've tried everything else," or "Maybe it's the only way left when everyone else hates you," or "Maybe it's the only way."

# Forward Day by Day

*Saturday, March 17, 2001*

⁜

*Since all have sinned and fall short of the glory of God;*
*they are now justified by his grace as a gift,*
*through the redemption that is in Christ Jesus.*
— ROMANS 3:23-24

By now, you know me: I get more than a little hung up on saying any way is the only way. Can't a person receive forgiveness and redemption directly from God? Does it have to be through Jesus?

It did for Buddy.

Buddy has been in prison since 1968. He didn't figuratively kill his brother as I did; he literally killed his own brother and another man. After entering prison, he became infamous for his lack of hesitation when it came to killing.

He showed up at this prison for a short spell last fall. I heard through the grapevine that he'd "become" a Christian and was going to give his testimony at the chapel, so I went.

I saw a man talk about living the first forty years of his life believing he was inherently bad—way too bad to turn to God. I saw a man smile and cry as he told how Jesus told him it was okay, to come to him anyway. Buddy's tears washed me. The light in his eyes lit my heart.

Did I believe that this man, the baddest of the bad, was forgiven? Yes, I knew it. But, you know, that wasn't really the miracle of that night. The miracle was that I finally knew I was forgiven. Thank you, God. Thank you, Jesus. Thank you, Buddy.

# Forward Day by Day

*Sunday, May 12, 2002 — Easter 7*

✠

*He brings forth prisoners into freedom.*
— Psalm 68:6

It's tempting. I'd love to believe they're talking about me when they use the word prisoner in the Bible. I've corresponded with quite a few people, and I'm always amazed at the number of comparisons between me and Joseph or anyone who "did time" in the Bible.

The main difference is that they were innocent, and I am as guilty as anyone who ever sat for a mug shot. I'm not being sold into slavery by a pack of corrupt brothers, and I'm not being persecuted because I'm a Christian.

I'm in prison because I killed a very precious young man named Bart. I am guilty of taking a life I cannot replace. No matter how long I stay in, no matter if I were to die for my transgression against Bart, his family, and God, no matter what, I cannot undo what I did. All I can do is try to live. And hope. Meanwhile, every time I see the word prisoner, I want to think I'm like Joseph or Paul. But I'm not. I'm guilty. It's important we all remember that.

Those people deserved to be out of prison. I don't deserve it. It doesn't mean I won't get out someday but, should I ever, it'll be undeserved, unadulterated grace. Mercy. Forgiveness. Light.

It's all I've got coming. And it's so much more than I can describe, much less deserve.

# Forward Day by Day

✠

*Even though I was formerly a blasphemer,*
*a persecutor and a man of violence...*
— 1 TIMOTHY 1:13A

At the height of my drug use, I would curse God. When I first came to prison, I would glare at men worshiping. The night I killed Bart was another in a string of drunken fights that had begun to become routine.

Two out of three ain't bad. I'm still a blasphemer and persecutor. Granted, I'm not as bad as I once was, but I've still got a way to go.

Blasphemer. I get mad when things don't go my way. Since I know from experience that sometimes I don't know what's best and I hardly ever understand God's ways, it's blasphemy not to trust him. I might not get what I want, but basing my relationship with God on what's in it for me is what I need to grow out of.

Persecutor. I don't like fundamentalists or legalists. People who get caught up in what everyone believes about Jesus as opposed to whether they believe in him at all seem to miss the point. People so sure of what they believe are also too sure about what I should believe. I resent that. In doing so, I become like them, and, suddenly, I know what's best for them.

Later in the reading from 1 Timothy, it says, "Christ Jesus came into the world to save sinners." That's good because I still need saving. From myself more than anything.

# Forward Day by Day

*Friday, July 5, 2002*

✠

*Deliver me, O LORD, from evildoers.*
— PSALM 140:1

It's important to me that you know exactly who you're dealing with. Of course you know I've killed another man. In spite of my efforts to keep Bart from becoming a nameless, statistically labeled "victim," the bottom line is that he's gone, and I did that. That in itself is enough. There's more.

When I was a young teenager, I would force my younger brother to smoke weed with me and my friends, so he wouldn't tell on me. It was more than twenty years before he was able to write and tell me he'd just celebrated his first year completely drug-free.

That's not the only time I got someone started using drugs. One time, during one of my attempts at college, I got a young man started using a needle. Five years later, I saw him in prison.

I've sold drugs to people who I knew needed to be spending their money on food for their kids. I've stolen money from my mom and my brother and embezzled money from my aunts. I'm embarrassed and humbled to say they still send me money today.

These are but a few of the *CliffsNotes* from a troubled and tumultuous past. There's more.

If you know me today, you're likely to say, "He's got a good heart." In fact, some people do. I can't help but remember it's the same heart I've always had. It's capable of atrocities. And it's capable of participating in miracles.

---

I Will: Persevere

# Forward Day by Day

*Friday, July 26, 2002 — Parents of the Blessed Virgin Mary*

✠

*Do not withhold your compassion from me.*
— PSALM 40:12

It's been over a week since I experienced that magical and yet oh-so-real taste of forgiveness. It's been over a month since Bart's cousin wrote and bathed me in that same light. There have been other times, contemplating the grass or watching a sparrow hop around, that God has told me I'm forgiven. Still, I struggle with that unfathomable truth.

A few weeks ago, I got to see some pictures of Bart's grave. A person I knew was going down there to visit it and leave some flowers and asked if I'd like a picture. They know how I struggle with finding the place between forgiveness and forgetfulness and thought this may help. I've seen lots of tombstones but never one that I was directly responsible for.

As I stared at the picture, the granite reminder of my actions, I tried to remember what it felt like to be forgiven. The best I could come up with was a personal oath not to forget this picture. As far as my life may go, I can't leave that behind. It wouldn't be right. It's a part of who I am. As much as people need to hear about forgiveness, they also need to hear about real life. And death.

Hidden between that tombstone's granite face and the light's illumination and shadows, lies the balance.

# In Transition

*Saturday, February 28, 2004*

✠

*Then I acknowledged my sin to you,*
*and did not conceal my guilt.*
*I said, "I will confess my transgressions to the LORD."*
*Then you forgave me the guilt of my sin.*
— PSALM 32:5

It is an understatement to say I have a mischievous side. Part of me is small-minded and mean. Let someone cut me off in traffic or, worse, get behind me at night with their bright lights on and there will sometimes come a stream of profanity that sounds a lot more indicative of the angry, scared, and hurting young man who went to prison in 1986 than it does of the author and speaker who is also on the staff of a drug and alcohol treatment center.

Friends in prison used to tease me, saying that I was "diabolically opposed." They said that there were two people inside me, fighting for control of the real me. I do not know if it is that severe, but I do know that I have thoughts and feelings that I am glad never manifest themselves as actions.

I remember one time when I was about six or seven. We lived in Wyoming on a Shoshoni reservation. I had a Daisy BB gun and had been out shooting it. One of the things I discovered was that the neighbor's horses would jump and buck if I shot them. This seemed fun, and, despite the fact I knew it was wrong, I could not seem to get enough.

One day I shot a horse in the eye. I could tell I had done something much worse than I had been doing by shooting at them in the first place.

The horse began to swing its head wildly, and its whinny was painful. Scared, I ran back to my house determined never to do that again.

Later, my dad came to me. "Son? Did you shoot the neighbor's horse in the eye?"

I shook my head no.

"Son?"

No, again. This time, weaker.

"Son, tell me the truth."

As I confessed, sobbing, the thing I discovered was that he already knew. Punishment included, it felt good to be cleansed of this horrible secret.

These days, as an adult, I laugh when I catch myself going to God to confess a wrong, thinking that I am telling God something that he does not already know. Confession is good for the heart and soul. It is cleansing. Lest we be confused about this, let's remember we are not doing God any favors. Confession is for us, not God. God already knows. But confession without penance makes for an unsatisfying absolution. We will not feel completely cleansed and forgiven by God unless we make penitent restitution to the person (or to the persons, or to the horse) we have hurt. The question is, do we know how to genuinely say, "I am sorry. I will make amends"? In that way confession is complete, and God is greatly pleased.

# In Transition

*Monday, April 5, 2004*

✠

*The sacrifice of God is a troubled spirit;*
*a broken and contrite heart, O God, you will not despise.*
— PSALM 51:18

Sometimes, people will contact me and ask me to talk to someone they know. Usually it will have something to do with a drug or alcohol problem. I never say no, but what I do say is this: "Sure, I will talk with them but I have got to tell you, until so-and-so is ready, there is not a PhD or MD or any other expert that is going to help them. Likewise, when so-and-so is ready, a monkey with flashcards will suffice."

That's sometimes construed as callous or even aloof. You see, I know without a doubt that when a person reaches the state of existence described above, there is nothing that will stop that person from getting better. Likewise, I know that until a person reaches that state of teachability, there is little or nothing I, or anyone else, can do for them. That includes God.

Sure, I suppose God could intervene without being invited. After all, God is God. But, as we have the freedom of choice, we do not have to accept it. With many of us, it is only after we have tried every other way—sometimes dozens of times each—that we are willing to say, "I can't do it. Will you help me?"

Then, the most important part, right after asking for help, is doing whatever it is that's suggested in reply to our request for help. Otherwise, our mouths are saying, "Help" while our actions are saying, "Never mind. I've got it."

It doesn't have to be drugs and alcohol that bring us to this state of malleability. Anytime our choices bring us to a place where there's not one more way to turn, we can know the condition the psalmist talks of. When we know that condition, there is always hope, for oftentimes it is there, in that most vulnerable state, that God comes.

A friend of mine would always say, "My best thinking got me in prison, doing a life sentence. Doing the very best I knew, this is what happened. So, I figured, what have I got to lose by listening and trying another way?"

What do we have to lose? Our life. But isn't at least one of the lessons of Easter about losing our life so that we may gain it?

Finally, for me, it is a state of freedom not to have to pretend I am anything more than a pitiful man who has made a pitiful mess out of a lot of his life. I bring this to God, daily.

# Forward Day by Day

*Friday, April 8, 2011*

✠

*For I am convinced that neither death, nor life, nor angels,*
*nor rulers, nor things present, nor things to come, nor powers,*
*nor height, nor depth, nor anything else in all creation,*
*will be able to separate us from the love of God*
*in Christ Jesus our Lord.*
— ROMANS 8:38-39

In addition to having lived my own story, I have worked with folks who have torn their own lives (and the lives of those close to them) to pieces through addiction and its accompanying clouds of fear. Coming out the other side with them to stand with our faces in the sun helps me feel the weight of this statement from Romans.

For me, the love of God in Christ Jesus doesn't evoke mission statements or formulas for personal salvation, prosperity, or favor. Instead, it creates a place of radical inclusiveness embodied in Christ Jesus and seen in all of creation.

I recently saw the movie *Crazy Heart*. In it, Jeff Bridges plays an alcoholic country singer whose self-destructive lifestyle has led to broken marriages and a failed career. When he finally hits bottom, he seeks help.

After the show, one of my friends asked me, "What's the message?" I couldn't even muster an answer. Later, he called me and said, "We don't get back what we've lost; we get what we never had."

# Forward Day by Day

*Friday, April 15, 2011*

✠

*[Judas] said this not because he cared about the poor,*
*but because he was a thief.*
— JOHN 12:6A

"When do you think they'll let me go home?"

Outwardly, the young man seemed as normal as anyone; yet, something had happened to bring him to a psychiatric hospital. I wasn't aware of his particulars, so I asked, "What happened?"

He explained how things simply got out of hand, went from nothing out of the ordinary, to slightly skewed, to "uh-oh," to crisis. Next thing he knew, he was in the emergency room. It is a more common scenario than you might think. We see a number of people for whom things seemed just fine last month, last week, or yesterday.

In light of this, painting Judas all bad ignores his—and our own—humanity. I promise you, Judas had some good in him. Despite religion's need to paint Judas as a puppet in a preordained saga, it is more believable that Judas was like the young man in the psychiatric hospital—things just got out of hand.

The best among us innately accommodate a capacity for the worst, and the reverse is also true: the worst are capable of the best.

In a world without this paradox, there would be no need for a savior.

# Forward Day by Day

*Thursday, February 6, 2014*

⨁

*When many of his disciples heard it, they said,*
*"This teaching is difficult. Who can accept it?"*
— JOHN 6:60

"**B**o, I'm scared. I'm not sure I can do this."

The words are not always exactly the same but the sentiment is. Someone is on their way out of rehab or the hospital, and, looking at what lies ahead, they are overwhelmed.

Their doubt and fear is understandable. Oftentimes in recovery, people are told to not worry, they only have to change one thing: everything. Later in their journey, this becomes tongue-in-cheek banter, but early on it can be paralyzing.

Truly, who among us can or wants to change everything? It is no surprise that recovery statistics are so low. (At least on the first try.)

Early on in my journey, someone said that only two people in my group of twenty or so would make it. Thankfully, I thought to myself that I was going to be one of those two. Sadly, I believe most people automatically assume they'll be one of the eighteen.

One day I was complaining about how hard it was to change habits built up over decades. A man who had many years ahead of me on this path looked at me, smiled, and said, "Son, if it were easy, everyone would do it."

# Forward Day by Day

*Friday, February 14, 2014*

✠

*You have laid me in the depths of the Pit,*
*in dark places, and in the abyss.*
— PSALM 88:7

At one time in my life, I could and would tell you that the shape my life was in—pitiful, at best—was someone, or something, else's fault. Truth is, I had done it.

The psalmist goes on to write: "I am in prison and cannot get free. My sight has failed me because of trouble."

Although I was physically in prison, its lowness and darkness was nothing compared to the state of being me. Not living up to the person God created and my parents raised was as low and dark a place as in all creation. Even worse, I couldn't see two things: one, I had caused it; two, I didn't even know I was in a low and dark place.

That's how it is with addiction to alcohol and other drugs—while your life is systematically extinguished, you think everything is okay as long as you can get, and stay, high. The only problem most of us had was that people wouldn't leave us alone.

Thank God they didn't, and thank God I finally realized the people "bothering" me were the ones who loved me.

The good news? Recovery is possible.

# CHAPTER 3

# Proclaim

*Will you proclaim by word
and example the Good News
of God in Christ?*

I will, with God's help.

# The Value of Toys

*Release: Meditations from Prison, Day 3, 1995*

✛

*And he said to them, "Take care!*
*Be on your guard against all kinds of greed;*
*for one's life does not consist*
*in the abundance of possessions."*
— Luke 12:15

Have you seen the bumper sticker that says, "He who dies with the most toys wins?" Before I came to prison I was like that. I wanted stuff.

In prison, my belongings consist of a thirteen-inch TV, a few clothes, shoes, books, and a small radio. I make $27 a month at my job. My food is shoveled through a wooden window, on a dull plastic tray, by an unhappy, apathetic man three times a day. It's usually cold. I live in a tiny eight-by-ten-feet cinder-block cell with another prisoner.

All in all, I don't have a lot. If I were still hung up on how much stuff I had (and I was for a while), happiness and contentment would be mighty elusive.

Out of this meager existence, I've come to learn what possessions are important. It's certainly not material goods. It's spiritual goods.

Jesus told his followers that no matter how many toys they die with, they're not taking any with them—wherever they go.

Jesus is a king. He is God's son. He is our Savior. He is the most influential man who ever lived. He was born into material poverty, but he's spiritually rich.

Lord, help me to be rich like that.

# Giving Up—to Win

*Release: Meditations from Prison, Day 22, 1995*

✛

*"God opposes the proud, but gives grace to the humble."*
*Submit yourselves therefore to God...*
*Let your laughter be turned into mourning*
*and your joy into dejection.*
*Humble yourselves before the Lord*
*and he will exalt you.*
— JAMES 4:6B-7A, 9B-10

Did you know that, as it was being formed, the program of Alcoholics Anonymous was almost called the James Club? It was. Many of the principles that millions of recovered alcoholics and addicts follow as they stay sober come from the Book of James.

Those who have been down in the gutter, literally or figuratively, and have risen from it, can attest to the fact that it was out of that mournful and dejected state they came to know the full measure of God's grace.

The paradoxical first step of AA reads: "We admitted we were powerless over alcohol—that our lives had become unmanageable."

It's paradoxical because out of this powerless and hopeless state we are able to rise and find so much power and hope. It doesn't make sense. But it works.

When you're lying on the bottom, whether it be a result of drugs, alcohol, or just life's pains, there is only one way to look. Up. He'll be there. I guarantee it.

# Forward Day by Day

✠

*Indeed, some are last who will be first,*
*and some are first who will be last.*
— LUKE 13:30

It was graduation night. May 1981. I had on a purple robe. So did all the others. Everyone looked the same. Except for the gold braids. Each student who was in the top 20 percent scholastically had a golden braid on one shoulder. It set them apart—head of the line. It was unspoken: they were the most likely to succeed. They were "first."

Today, one of them is an accountant. Another, an advertising executive. Almost without exception, every one of them did very well with their lives. They succeeded. Almost all of them. Except one.

Since that night, he's been a low-bottom drunk and hopeless junkie, he's been penniless, he's been a liar, he's been a cheater, he's been a thief, he's lived in slums, and for eleven of those sixteen years he's been in prison for killing another person.

I was first, now I'm last.

Or, am I? I have something today that is unshakable. I don't even fully understand what it is, but I know it has to do with love.

Jesus is talking about order—first, last, last, first—but I don't think this message has anything to do with us getting in a line. The message is: there is no line. God loves every one of us exactly the same. A lot.

The kingdom is now, and each of us is wearing a gold braid.

# Forward Day by Day

*Wednesday, March 25, 1998 — The Annunciation*

✤

*Then Mary said, "Here am I, the servant of the Lord;*
*let it be with me according to your word."*
— LUKE 1:38A

What would your answer have been? I probably would have said, "That's a fantastic idea, Mr. Angel, but if we do it your way, then I'll miss working out tomorrow and, also, I had plans for this weekend. It's not that I don't want to, it's just that, well, you know, I'm pretty busy. So could we do it my way?"

A few days ago, I mentioned being more at peace than I've ever been. Ever. I'm also the happiest I've ever been. Healthiest. Most free. Most successful. Most grateful. I think I'm starting to realize God's will in my life, accepting that he wants good for me.

Thing is, I wouldn't have picked this route. I would've opted for an easier, softer way. There are moments when I know with a divine certainty that there was no other path for me except the one I've walked. In reality, all of the wrong choices, mistakes, and painful moments have been steps in this journey. For this reason, my prayer these days is:

God,

Whatever.

Thank you.

It's not a foot-dragging, whining whatever. It's a whatever from a person who is beginning to realize that God has bigger and better plans than he does.

Mary said the same thing.

---

I Will: Proclaim

# Forward Day by Day

*Monday, March 30, 1998*

✠

*Into your hands I commit my spirit;*
*for you have redeemed me, O LORD, O God of truth.*
— PSALM 31:5

Shame. Trap. Hate. Worthless. Affliction. Anguish. Soul. Enemy. Distress. Sorrow. Groaning. Bones. Contempt. Dread. Dead. Broken. Slander. Terror. Conspire. Plot. Cried. Wicked. Grave. Lying. Pride. Contempt. Arrogantly. Accusing. Besieged. Alarm.

Some of the words from Psalm 31. Palette number one.

Refuge. Righteousness. Rescue. Strong. Fortress. Rock. Lead. Guide. Free. Redeem. Truth. Trust. Glad. Rejoice. Love. Spacious. Merciful. Deliver. Shine. Unfailing. Great. Goodness. Shelter. Presence. Dwelling. Safe. Praise. Wonderful. Mercy. Help. Preserves. Faithful. Heart. Hope. More words from the same psalm. Palette number two.

Quite the contrast, isn't it? Night and Day. Death and Life. The human condition. Read over both lists again. Slowly. Let the words from each palette roll off your tongue. Taste them. Take your time.

Today, and every day from this moment on, is your empty canvas. You have a paint brush in your hand and life is your picture to paint. The good news is that you get to choose which palette.

Go ahead. Dip your brush. Either palette.

Hint number one: Don't worry if you mess up and paint an awful picture. You can start over at any time.

Hint number two: you can ask for help.

# Forward Day by Day

*Saturday in Easter Week, April 18, 1998*

✠

*I shall not die, but live,*
*and declare the works of the LORD.*
— PSALM 118:17

M ost of my life, I've thought that life was temporary and death was forever. That train of thought left me scared to die and scared to live. I'm not sure that I have even a halfway grasp on this eternal life thing, but I do know that with death comes life, and that each time something dies, I am left with a deeper awareness of life's infinite potential.

With the death of my drug addiction came a million forms of life. Each time some self-centeredness dies in me, more capacity to care about someone other than me is born. Every time a lie dies unspoken, truth lives. When a resentment becomes a compassionate understanding, life becomes a bit more forever. As I walk through the fears in my life and discover them to be False Events Appearing Real, they are replaced with faith and love.

Even the times I felt like I was dying were transformed into beautiful new growth.

I have come to believe that deaths are opportunities for new births. New life after death is what lasts forever and reigns supreme. This has empowered me to live my life in a brand-new way. I am no longer afraid of dying, and he has opened up an eternity of living.

I Will: Proclaim

# Bart's Cousin

*God Is Not In the Thesaurus:*
*Stories from an Oklahoma Prison, 1999*

⊹

*And the Word became flesh...*
— JOHN 1:14

*How are y'all doin'? My name is Bo Cox. I'd like to thank you for coming to prison today. I hope it turns out to be a good experience. You guys look a little uptight. You okay? Well, let me tell ya somethin': I'm more scared of you than you are of me. So, if I appear a little nervous, please bear with me.*

*I grew up in a small town in southeastern Oklahoma, not far from where you guys live. As a matter of fact, we used to play ya'll in basketball and baseball. I guess we probably still do, although I wouldn't know; I've been in here for a while.*

I was speaking to the Latta, Oklahoma, senior class of 1992. I belong to a group called Straight Talk, and that's what we do, talk straight. We conduct tours of the prison, followed by intense question and answer sessions. Area schools, churches, civic groups come on a regular basis. We share our life experiences with the young and, sometimes, not so young. The way I see it, there's a two-fold advantage. Maybe, we can save some kids from making the same mistakes we've made, and the public has the chance to see that not everyone in prison is a raging, maniacal, developmentally retarded high school dropout and sociopathic loser.

*I don't know how it is in Latta today, but in Coalgate, in 1978, smoking weed and drinking were it. Again, I don't know about you guys, but I'm tellin' ya, the first time I got high I fell in love. Man, it felt so good. Those of you with smiles on your faces know what I'm talking about. I thought I had found the way. I was just fifteen, and no one, I'm telling you, no one, was going to stop me from getting high. You guys know. I don't expect you to raise your hand or anything, but I do hope you listen. 'Cause, see, y'all, as good as it feels, and believe me—I know how good it feels—there's more.*

More than once, I've seen the teachers' shocked expressions as I've admitted to students how good it feels to get high. But honesty is the best policy. Grown-ups didn't shoot straight with me. They told horror stories about the dangers of dope. It was obvious they'd never tried it, and after I did my own research, I found out they'd lied. I didn't go blind, start stealing or foaming at the mouth, or put an infant in the dryer.

The truth was I felt good. I was cool, confident. Coolness and confidence are elusive for a fifteen-year-old. That's one of the reasons this is a very big thing. Drugs feel good. That's the truth. That's why people do them.

If I don't tell the truth, what's going to happen when someone goes ahead and tries drugs? I become a liar and what I've said becomes a lie. So, it's best to tell the truth. Besides, I don't want them to miss the rest of my story.

*You know what? From the time I was fifteen until I graduated, I got loaded every day. Oh sure, on the surface, everything seemed cool. After all, I wasn't stealing to support my habit. Most of my friends were getting high. I hadn't graduated past weed and alcohol, so, in my head, I really didn't have a drug problem. Still, there were some people who were concerned about me and what they perceived as a problem. But every time someone approached me, I'd get defensive and point out to them why I didn't have a drug problem. If I've got a drug problem, why haven't I been kicked off the team? Why am I still in the honor society? Or, I'd look 'em straight in the eye and say, Me? Drugs? Well, yeah, I drink a little, but not all the time. I smoke pot occasionally, who doesn't? I'd never mess with hard drugs. Does that sound familiar to anyone in this room? Again, you don't have to raise your hand. Just listen. I've got a question for you. Say you were an alcoholic. I'm not saying you are, just imagine that you were. Would you tell anyone?*

Hardly anyone would raise a hand on that question. Why?

One reason is those kids have been told one way or another that there is something wrong with being an alcoholic or an addict.

Being an alcoholic or an addict doesn't make one bad, yet we believe it does. So, I ask them to give me their definition of an alcoholic or addict. Usually it's "Someone who drinks all the time." "Someone whose clothes are all wrinkled and they smell." "Someone who steals to support a habit." "Someone who can't hold a job." "Someone with a beer belly." "Someone really skinny."

Sometimes alcoholics or addicts fit stereotypes. More often they don't. That's not the point—what an alcoholic or addict looks like. The point is that we attach a dark cloud of shame to alcoholism and addiction so that even if a person discovers he or she is one and wants help, most are ashamed to ask for it.

*Hey, guys, guess what? I'm an alcoholic. I'm also an addict. And you know what? That's not a bad thing. It simply means that I can't drink or use drugs at all because once I begin, I can't stop. It doesn't mean I'm a bad person. But you know what? I used to think it did. That was one of the reasons my life got really, really bad before I was desperate enough to look at the possibility of my being an alcoholic and addict. The bottom line? Once I admitted it, I discovered it was nothing to be ashamed of. It doesn't mean that I'm a cheater, liar, thief, loser, drunk, or junkie. All it means is that I can't drink or use drugs.*

That usually gets their attention. Here is a relatively together-looking guy, in good physical shape, happy, well-groomed, with a glow in his eye, definitely not chemically induced. It feels good to see them look at one another, raise their eyebrows. It changes their perception. Someday, if they ever discover they need help, it may save their life.

*How many of you guys play baseball? Basketball? How about you girls? Basketball? Softball? Are any of you in the honor society? Would you believe I lettered four years in football, three in basketball, and two in baseball? Would you believe that during senior year, I was a captain of a football team ranked fifth in the state? I was in the honor society. All through high school, I went steady with the smartest girl in our school.*

What really scares me is that just as people have misconceptions about alcoholism and addiction, others are as ignorant as I once was concerning prisons. I grew up between McAlester and Stringtown—two of Oklahoma's biggest prisons. It was no big deal to drive by the crews of white-shirted, tattooed men on the sides of the highways, as they picked up trash and cut weeds, while the armed guards on horseback made sure they didn't escape. Although I felt something disturbing, I wouldn't look twice as I drove by the huge, draconian complexes. Just about every highway sported a sign saying: WARNING: HITCHHIKERS MAY BE ESCAPING CONVICTS.

I was used to prisons. I knew a lot of people who worked there; however, I didn't know any of the men who lived there. I knew they must be different from me or any of my friends. I assumed they were men who were born bad, did bad things, and when they turned eighteen were sent to prison.

The biggest mistake young visitors (people of all ages) can make is to walk out thinking they're different from me. They're not. Every time I talk to a school group, I look back and can see myself sitting in the back row.

*So, guys, I graduated from high school with a formidable drug habit. Now, I didn't know that I was already out of control. I still believed that I could handle drugs. And, it wasn't just beer and weed anymore. Nope. When I started, I'd swore that being an athlete, I'd never do anything harder than drinking and smoking weed. By the time I had graduated from high school, I'd tried everything—pills, crank, coke, snorting, shooting—*

*anything that would get me high. There wasn't a drug I wouldn't try. I went to college. Twice. Dropped out both times. I tried work. Quit every job I got. Of course, none of these things was ever my fault. It just happened.*

*By this time, a couple years after I'd graduated from high school, I was in the midst of a full-blown amphetamine addiction. For the next year and a half, I was a speed junkie. When it all caught up with me and I got in trouble, I weighed one hundred and thirty-five pounds and looked like a skeleton.*

This never fails to get their attention. Looking at me, it is hard to conceive. Here's this guy, almost two hundred pounds, healthy as a horse, happy and smiling. It just doesn't add up. He was a junkie? They begin to pay closer attention. This group was no exception. I noticed them sitting up in their seats...looks of amazement, distaste, pity... everything.

*I was in trouble, busted with a bunch of my friends, and we all landed in jail. Even though we swore allegiance to one another, the minute we landed in jail, everyone started to tell on one another. All the romance and exciting outlaw stuff went out the window. It was dog-eat-dog. Sitting in jail, I realized my life was a mess. But I missed the point, even though I had an awakening. I decided I had a problem with hard drugs, and I would have to do what it took to leave them alone. But stupidly I thought I could still handle drinking and smoking pot. Those things were okay. Everyone did them, and I'd never gotten in real trouble.*

It's not the easiest thing in the world to tell a group of strangers how stupid you were. But it's important for two reasons: first, it's a perfect illustration of the insanity of alcoholism and addiction, and second, I see people nod when I say that hard drugs are dangerous, yet look the other way when it comes to alcohol and marijuana, especially alcohol.

Thinking that alcohol is different, okay, acceptable, is one of the biggest mistakes I made. I want every person who hears me speak, especially those who nod their heads in approval when I tell them how I laid down the "hard stuff" in favor of "just drinking," to know exactly how grave that misconception is.

*For the next few months, life was as good as it had ever been for me. It's true: I wasn't strung out on drugs anymore. I even had a job. Even though I drank heavily and smoked pot every day, people, myself included, thought I was getting it together. On July 25, 1996, after a day of driving a dump truck, I got off work and me and a few of my buddies started drinking—just like any other Friday.*

If I were the least bit nervous when I began, this is the point my nervousness rises to new heights. My voice quivers, my heart begins to race, I start to sweat. July 26, 1986, isn't easy to live with, and my body protests when I relive it. Every time I tell the story it gets a little easier but never easy enough.

*So after drinking all afternoon, all evening, and all night, I found myself on Main Street about two o'clock in the morning. I'm not sure how it all happened, but I know it started when Bart and I started calling each other names. That's right, calling each other names. Pretty stupid. I got out of my truck, and we started to fight. Everyone gathered around, egging us on, hollering, cussing—you know how it is in a fight when everyone is drunk. Before I knew what was happening, I'd stopped fighting the first guy and another guy had jumped in. At this stage in the game, I realized I was outnumbered, and I had better get my tail out of there. So, I did. I left.*

*This should be the end of this story. But it's not because, you see, when I got a few blocks down the street, I started thinking about how everyone was going to call me a sissy the next day for leaving the fight and letting those guys run me off. This is an important point. How many of you guys, girls too, when you get in a fight, fight because you're tough? How many of you fight because you're afraid of what people will say if you don't? Let me tell you guys something: I've not once been in a fight where I wasn't scared to death. I'm not just talking about being scared of getting beat up.*

*Thing is, I've always been more scared of what people would think about me if I didn't fight.*

You should see the faces on the kids. They understand. There aren't many of them who are ready to raise their hands and say, "Yeah, the only reason I fight is I'm scared everyone will think I'm a sissy if I don't." They don't have to raise their hands and say it. I can see it in their eyes. In the way they drop their heads, look at the floor, and shuffle their feet.

*So after driving down the road a few blocks, I turned around and went back and called everyone names as I drove by. They all jumped in their cars and followed me out of town. I pulled off on a dirt road and got a baseball bat out of my pickup. I was gonna show them I wasn't scared.*

Suddenly I heard hysterical sobbing in the back row. It was a girl I'd noticed staring at me. She had her head buried in her hands, and her small body was being racked by loud, uncontrollable sobs. I couldn't stop watching her. I saw her teacher rush to her side. So did her principal and a best friend. Everyone was watching the little circle around her. I became so distracted I lost track of what I was saying, wound up the story and sat down. I wanted to disappear. I'd had people cry before when I was talking. It's understandable. This is a sad, tragic story and unsettling. Still, I wondered what had upset her so much.

I looked at her, and when she finally met my gaze, I saw something that scared me. I knew. I knew what she was coming to tell me, what the essence of her message was going to be.

"Bo, that little girl is the cousin of the guy you killed."

I don't have the words to describe what I felt at that moment. Scared is an understatement. Sorry is so inadequate.

"She wants to talk with you."

I was paralyzed. My friends told me later that I turned as white as a sheet. I'd been in prison for six years. I'd slept in the same rooms with men who had murdered, robbed, raped, assaulted. Not once had I been as terrified as I was of this little seventeen-year-old girl, who simply wanted to sit down and talk.

"Bo, do you want to? You don't have to."

Yes, I did.

All of us—the teacher, the principal, the best friend, Bart's cousin, and I—went off to a quiet corner and sat down in a circle. Someone started talking, trying to mediate. All I could do was sit there, head hanging, and wring my hands, trying to muster the courage to raise my head and look the girl in the eye.

After a moment, I managed to look up. She said, "I just want you to know that I don't hate you."

"Thank you."

Time was suspended. Everyone else tried to fill the silence. I can't remember what they said. I could hear them, nodded my head, struggled like a drowning person to find some words. I couldn't.

Words weren't necessary. As everyone got up to leave, she smiled. It wasn't a pretty, everything-is-better-now, I'm glad-we-had-this-talk, now-I'm-okay smile, but a smile full of hurt and confusion and forgiveness and love. It must've been difficult to smile that smile, and it must have felt good.

In that tear-streaked smile, I began to get a glimpse, literally and figuratively, of God. It's understandable that she could hate me. Yet she didn't. Even though it feels good and even though I want it, I don't feel like I deserve her forgiveness, but there are moments when I am able to accept it and know it.

Somewhere in the middle of all that, there lies an elusive and a very sacred truth: the word can become flesh. I know. The word was a petite, brown-eyed, black-haired girl that day. The word was hurt and scared. The Word was, and is, alive.

# Friends and Ice Cream

*God Is Not In the Thesaurus:*
*Stories from an Oklahoma Prison, 1999*

✛

*God is able from these stones to raise up children to Abraham.*
— MATTHEW 3:9B

On a Saturday night in February 1997, six of us were eating ice cream in a tiny prison cell. By the half gallon, we ate rocky road, triple chocolate, bowls and bowls—laughing and cutting up like boys at a slumber party.

Except we're not boys. Four are serving time for killing, one for assault, one for manufacturing and selling drugs. Our sentences add up to two life sentences and over a hundred years. So far we've been in prison a total of forty-three years. If you judge us from the descriptions filed in our records, you wouldn't want us in your neighborhood. We're hard-core, long-term, violent offenders.

Some introductions:

Fifteen years ago, Jerry killed a man in a drunken brawl. That's not the reason he's my hero. He's my hero because he has taught me that happiness, contentment, and joy come from inside, not outside. I look up to him and respect him. When I'm hurting, I go to him. He's a person in whom I see peace. He's been a lot of things in his life: drifter and doper, drunk and down-and-out. Today, after five years of sobriety, he's a computer programmer, leader, helper, and hero. He's found a design for living that works, and his life is all about sharing that with others. He's my John the Baptist.

Skip's my cell partner. Before he started drinking, he was an avid and accomplished athlete, a good scholar, an all-around good kid. Once he started drinking, it progressed rapidly, and the years turned into a blur. He was a freshman at Oklahoma State University, five years ago, when he shot and killed one of his best friends during an alcoholic blackout. For most people, that sounds like a cop-out, a way to avoid owning responsibility for one's actions. To someone who knows what it's like to drink when you swear you're not going to and then, once you start, not to remember anything after the first couple of drinks, it's reality. Many a night Skip and I sit up until the wee hours, and I listen to the young man try to make sense out of his life. It's been a blessing to watch him uncover the forgiveness for himself that he needs. In the process, he's taught me to find a balance between accepting responsibility for my own actions and at the same time not letting my past prevent me from claiming my future.

If I had a penny for each time David has told me how much his friends mean to him, I could buy my way out of prison. Drugs and alcohol were a way of life for David at a very early age. A simple progression led to his arrest and conviction for drug sales. He's never known anything else, until he came here. He's the father of two little boys, and when he talks about them, tears come. You may well say, "If those boys were so important to him he wouldn't have come to prison." There is truth in that statement. But when addiction is part of the equation, logic, the ought-to's, and should-have's go out the window. When David tells me how special we are to him, I wonder if he knows how special he is to us. He's a rock.

Richard killed someone in a car wreck. He was messed up by pills and booze when it happened. But that's not what I think about when I think about Richard. I think about a summer evening two years ago. A group of us were sitting around talking about life, sobriety, God, prison, and an assortment of other subjects. Richard had recently arrived from another prison. Like me, he'd spent his first years in prison still looking for the answer in a joint, pill, or shot. He was sitting away from the group, on the outer edge, not really belonging. When he spoke, I got goosebumps. There was no denying the urgency or sincerity in his voice.

"I gotta clean up," he said. "I'm thirty-four years old, and I've failed at everything I've tried. It's gotta be answered prayer or something that I'm at this prison with you guys because I think this is my last chance, and I can't fail this time." He'll celebrate two years of sobriety this summer, and we'll eat ice cream at his birthday party, too.

And that's what we were doing in that cell: having a birthday party.

Daniel had been clean and sober one year. This guy had been in and out of treatment centers for a decade. Most of the people he knew, including himself, had written him off as a hopeless case. He just couldn't stay sober. He'd get a few months under his belt and, wham, find himself loaded and wondering how that happened. After more than a few years of that, he had come to believe that he probably couldn't do it. The first time I met him, I wondered. I don't wonder any more. In the past year, God has spoken volumes about life, hope, faith, love, and perseverance through Daniel. I've listened, and so has everyone else he knows.

These are my friends. They're the best friends I've ever had, and I'm a better friend because of them. We've cried and laughed together, learned together, sobered up together, grown up together. Most important, we've learned to love together. It's an amazing story, and sometimes I still can't believe it took place right here—in prison.

There we all were, eating ice cream, celebrating Daniel's birthday when, suddenly, David looked up from his bowl of ice cream and, with a quiver in his voice, said, "You know something? This is a miracle."

# Forward Day by Day

*Monday, March 5, 2001*

✠

*Take care that you do not forget the LORD your God.*
— DEUTERONOMY 8:11A

When I first sobered up, a friend helped me a lot by telling me this: 1) There is a God; and 2) It ain't you.

A few years ago, in the Texas governor's race, one of the candidates said this about an opponent: "He was born on third base and thought he'd hit a triple."

Really, it doesn't matter who coined these phrases or who they were aimed at; what matters is how far we've gotten in our respective journeys and how much credit we give ourselves for having gotten there.

Everything—the sun rising this morning; your breath causing your chest to rise and fall; the air in that breath; the color of your hair and the curl in it; the wind outside; the sparkle in the eyes of those you love; your sense of security; the birds in your yard; your accomplishments; a smile; a hug; a friendly word; your prayers this morning as well as the lives of the people you prayed for; the grass on your lawn; the food on your table tonight—is ultimately from our Creator.

It's not something to feel guilty about, living in the illusion that we are Masters of the Universe. It's a common affliction. Laugh at yourself and, when you head out today, remember to live this day in wonder and gratitude of the One who made this day possible. (Psst…it ain't you!)

# Forward Day by Day

✠

*For God so loved the world that he gave his only Son...*
— JOHN 3:16

Every time the ball sails through the uprights, you'll see it: JOHN 3:16. What does it mean? That everyone who doesn't believe in Jesus is going to hell? That seems to be the traditional consensus. That's the understanding I picked up, growing up in the Bible Belt.

What does the phrase "believe in Jesus" mean? Do I have to believe he was, simply, the son of God? Or, do I have to believe that when he was murdered, a whole new belief system superseded the old one? Do I have to believe that the kind and loving God I know and trust is really going to send a large portion of his family to a never-ending lake of fire?

How can I tell if someone believes in Jesus?

I've seen people who say Jesus every other word, but if you were deaf and couldn't hear them, you sure wouldn't identify them as Christians based on the way they live. I've seen people who, as far as I know, have never muttered his name. But the way they carry themselves is a flesh-and-blood embodiment of the one known as the Christ. It's confusing, playing the salvation game. While today's problems are enough in their own right, eternity still matters to me. Someone asked Jesus what was the most important thing to remember. He said for me to love God with all my heart, mind, and soul and to love my neighbor as myself. That'll keep me busy for eternity.

# Forward Day by Day

*Saturday, May 4, 2002*

✠

*Not everyone who says to me, "Lord, Lord,"*
*will enter the kingdom of heaven,*
*but only the one who does the will of my Father in heaven.*
— MATTHEW 7:21

In 1968 a seventeen-year-old with a pistol crawled out of his friend's car. He and the friend were high on gold paint. Gold paint was cheap, easy to get, and it would get you high enough to hallucinate. Within minutes, a man lay dead and his wife, wounded. The two young men went to Oklahoma's Death Row to await execution.

1972. The Supreme Court ruled the death penalty unconstitutional. All death sentences were commuted to life.

1989. I was in my third year of prison and had just arrived at this yard when I met Mike. It was his twenty-first year of incarceration. The first thing we did together was shoot speed. During the next year, we did that a lot.

1990. The two of us entered a drug and alcohol rehabilitation program.

Sometime today, I'll drop by his cell to play dominoes. Really, we'll talk. He's my mentor in the truest sense of the word. In fact, were it not for his presence in my life, I wouldn't be writing these words today. He's that much of an influence. He's not a writer, but he's the one who teaches me about Jesus.

How? I watch how he lives his life.

I Will: Proclaim

# Forward Day by Day

*Monday, June 10, 2002*

✠

*Whenever I am afraid, I will put my trust in you.*
— PSALM 56:3

Fifteen years ago, when I received my first notice of parole and saw the date, "June 2001," I thought, no way can I do fifteen years in this place. Yet, here I am. In less than ten days, I'll be going up for parole. It's a chance to: 1) Go home sometime this fall; 2) Stay in prison at least three more years.

Yesterday I talked with a friend who is helping me prepare for my hearing. He asked what I'll do if I don't make it. His question stopped me cold in my tracks. To tell the truth, I haven't been thinking about not making it. I've been wondering what it was going to be like making parole.

"Well, I suppose I'll pretty much do the same things I've been doing," I answered after a minute. After all, the only reason I've got a chance at parole is because of the miracles that have taken place in my life. Trying to participate in those miracles makes up a significant portion of my life and is part of the ongoing miracle that is my life.

I'm happy today. His question reminded me of how deep that truth is. I want out so bad, especially for my family. But, do you know what? It doesn't matter—my happiness is not contingent on this fence. The Most High's not afraid of galvanized chain link and razor wire and guard towers and guns.

When I trust the Most High, neither am I.

# Forward Day by Day

*Saturday, June 15, 2002*

⊹

*Who can stand before you when you are angry?*
— PSALM 76:7

God's anger, just like God, is way too big a concept for me to wrap my teeny human brain around. To let it go at overwhelming is enough. Besides, my anger is what I need to focus on and try to understand.

Fifteen years ago, next month, I did something in a moment of anger that ended one person's life and forever changed mine and others'. Although it had become a habit of mine, acting in anger, this particular tragedy only took a moment.

And, thing is, I just thought I was angry. Truth is, what I know as anger is really nothing more than fear. It was then, and it still is today. When I am scared, I react in anger. If I were to practice honesty in all my affairs, I wouldn't get angry anymore. Instead, I'd say, "Hey, this is scaring me. I'm afraid of (fill-in-the-blank)."

It's so difficult for me to admit I'm scared. I don't know if it's because I'm a man and somewhere along the way I picked up the erroneous idea that men aren't scared, or if it's because I'm in prison and it's certainly an unwritten rule in here: don't show fear. Maybe it's simply because I'm still immature and insecure and don't want anyone to think I'm as imperfect as God and I both know I am.

Whatever the reason, it is time I learned to live without fear. Without fear, I don't need anger. Without anger, God is love.

I Will: Proclaim

# Forward Day by Day

*Sunday, July 14, 2002 — 8 Pentecost*

✠

*So shall my word be that goes out from my mouth;*
*it shall not return to me empty.*
— ISAIAH 55:11A

My first day of school was terrifying. I can't remember the details, but I can still feel the fear that came with being dropped off at a building full of strangers. My mom gave me a pep talk, and I can recall the trust I felt in her words. I don't remember what she said, but it ended with, "I love you."

In spite of the fact I was too slow and didn't have a very strong arm, I wanted to play baseball. My friends, it seemed, could run so much faster, hit the ball so much farther, and throw it twice as hard. In a compassionate twist of fate, my dad was my first little league coach. Don't get me wrong: he was extra hard on me, but he also encouraged me every day: "You can do it."

During my tumultuous years, those words faded away.

Then, in what I like to call my second childhood, I began to face the world again. It was still scary. After all, this time it was in prison. Not only that, it looked even scarier than it had when I was a kid because, as a young adult, I'd spent so much time hiding from it. My parent's words were still there, waiting to pick me up again and help me live life.

You know, I've come to realize they had been there all along.

# Forward Day by Day

*Tuesday, July 16, 2002*

✛

*So do not become proud, but stand in awe.*
—ROMANS 11:20B

Soon, I go before the parole board for stage two. Hyperbole aside, this is my one shot at getting out of prison. The way the pendulum of public opinion and politics is swinging, there's no telling what could happen to prisons or the people in them in the next decade. It's difficult not to look at this as my only chance.

Desperation and fear make me want to say, "I deserve…"

Debb, my wife, reminds me that at least my family has a son to worry about. She told me not to become proud and to remember why I was standing before the board to begin with. That is a sobering reality I tend to dismiss when I get caught up in the outcome of parole.

When I let go of the outcome, humility and awe make me want to say, "Thank you, God." They make me more willing to simply be myself, no matter what, and able to see God in any and all places.

Life is good. It's better than I ever dreamed it could be. I can't describe my Creator—but I know God is real. I also know that to the extent I let God in my life, the better it gets. All the good in my life today is from that relationship.

In or out, that won't change.

I Will: Proclaim

# In Transition

✠

*My child, do not regard lightly the discipline of the Lord,*
*or lose heart when you are punished by him;*
*for the Lord disciplines those whom he loves.*
— HEBREWS 12:5B-6A

In Boy Scouts, in order to acquire the Swimming Merit Badge, you have to swim a mile. At least that is the way it was in the 1970s. At best, I was a mediocre swimmer. But I sure wanted that merit badge so I sat out to swim a mile. I employed a hybrid backstroke/dog-paddle-type method that kept me afloat long enough to complete the required distance. However, I was so slow that for the last half of my swim, I was the only kid left in the water. Everyone else had quit or finished. Some of them encouraged me, but the majority of kids sat on the bank and sang loud, jeering songs they made up about how slow I was.

That, and the fact that my dad was watching, only made me more determined to finish. When I finally crawled out of the water and stood, victorious, on the bank, their jeers turned to applause, and I felt like the world's best athlete. I thought, "I can do anything as long as I don't quit."

Years later, in what seemed like another lifetime, I looked toward what I saw as an unmanageable situation: serving a life sentence in prison. No way could I do this. Somewhere along the way—amidst the drugs and alcohol and general lack of discipline that generally accompanies them—I had forgotten what it felt like to simply follow through on something, to finish something I had started.

Somehow, I remembered how I felt that time as a kid when I looked out across that lake, and it seemed like an ocean. There was so much water. No way could I swim that far, I thought. But I got in and kept trying and then I tried some more when it became difficult. I didn't quit. One more kick. One more stroke. One more.

Was I still "in here"? The same boy who swam a mile, even though he really could not swim?

Last June, I got up one morning and wrote in my journal: "This is the first morning in seventeen years that I haven't woken in prison. There are no more metal doors slamming, no people standing outside my cell talking loudly while I tried to concentrate on reading or writing. All I can hear are birds and the cars on the highway almost a mile away."

I suspect you are like me. No, you may not have gone to prison or struggled through a mile swim but you have been through some difficult situations in your life. Quite possibly, they are more difficult than mine. Believing in and having a relationship with God has not spared you from discomfort. And, yet, if you are here today, reading these words on this page, you have made it. Despite the fact that life has not been exactly as you would have drawn it, you are still hanging in there. In fact, I suspect by this point you are doing more than hanging in there. I suspect you have come to appreciate whatever life happens to be. I suspect that you have stepped out, dripping onto your own personal shore and walked free from out of your own prisons enough times to know what I know.

And what is that, you ask? It is simply what I learned that day as I stepped up out of the lake: I can do anything as long as I do not quit.

In prison, I learned a crucial second part to that truth: No matter how much it feels like it, I am never alone. I never have been.

# In Transition

✠

*When Jesus realized that they were about to come and take him by force to*
*make him king, he withdrew again to the mountain by himself.*
— JOHN 6:15

By himself. Well, actually he was not ever really by himself. No
different from us, his Creator was always with him—and like us, a
part of him. Maybe, like us, he needed to get away from the rat race to
let that sink in. Maybe not. Maybe his retreat was entirely tactical and
had more to do with following what some believe was preordained than
it was practical and having do with his being human.

I prefer the human angle. One of the great truths I have stumbled
upon in my life is the awareness that I can be truly happy with me,
alone, locked in a closet (or a cell or on a mountain) with no one else
around. This bit of wisdom did not come easy. If you know anything
about me, you know that the tuition for this particular spiritual truth
was extremely costly—not just to me, either.

Today, however, I am left standing with a rock-solid comfort level
that I have never before experienced. Each day, the farther I travel this
road, I become more and more okay with me. This may not seem like
such a big deal unless you understood exactly how unhappy and ill at
ease I have been with myself most of my life. As far as I can remember,
I have not been happy, not deep down inside, unless someone else was
validating my worth. Even then, it was shallow and temporary.

This lack of self-worth and self-confidence led me down a path where
I would do most anything to gain acceptance, look cool, and appear like
I was not the most insecure guy I knew. Ironic, because I was.

---

On the night of July 26, 1986, when I killed Bart, I hit him with a bat because I wanted to show him and all the people watching that fight that I was not scared. I was willing to go to any length to appear as if I were not scared.

I had been doing that for years. My need to be perceived as more than I was led me to drink more than other people, do more drugs, act crazier, and do whatever it took to bolster my lack of self-love with others' approval.

Today, I am very thankful that I can go to the mountain to be alone. I can sit alone and be okay. Well, my Creator and me. Today, I am not uneasy in God's presence. I do not feel guilty for all the ways I still fall short in living up to a better ideal.

I still need others. In fact, I am very much a people person. But at the core of that is two basic beliefs: 1) God loves me and is with me; and 2) God knows everything about me and #1 is still true.

# Why Me?

*Praying Day by Day, 2009*

✛

*Some have entertained angels without knowing it.*
— HEBREWS 13:2B

Sometime around Thanksgiving, I took a young man to the Salvation Army to get some clothes. On the way there, he began to tell me about himself. That was helpful because he had never participated in the recreational activities at our treatment center, so I had not gotten to know him at all.

He talked of an abusive father and broken family. He told how they had no money growing up. Then he began to share his fears with me, especially his fear of participating in playground activities as a child because he wore thick glasses that, if broken, could not be replaced. That also explained why he had not participated in recreational activities at the treatment center, and it forced me to reexamine my assessment of him as merely lazy.

His eyes sparkled, and he held his head a little higher as he related to me that people had told him he was intelligent (to which I agreed and told him so), and that he wanted to do something with his life.

When we got to the Salvation Army, he grew excited and almost jumped out of the van before I had completely stopped, heading toward the store with long purposeful strides. I followed him in and tagged along as he picked out his clothes.

I noticed the care with which he was selecting his three pairs of pants and shirts, his shoes and jacket, and the pride with which he carried them to the register to check out.

Tears came to my eyes, and I ducked my head to gather myself together. I wasn't sure what or whom I was looking at. Nor could I answer the question: why me?

# Forward Day by Day

*Thursday, April 21, 2011 — Maundy Thursday*

✠

*They shall take some of the blood
and put it on the two doorposts
and the lintel of the houses in which they eat it.*
— EXODUS 12:7

Oklahoma had a prison-overcrowding problem and contracted with private prison corporations to house thousands of prisoners. (It didn't work—Oklahoma still has near-record overcrowding.) For months, prison staff would come in the middle of the night and gather people out of their cells, chain them, and lead them out.

I remember hearing the doors open and the chains rattle. I would creep to my door to sneak a look, all the while holding my breath, hoping it wouldn't be our door they opened. It was simply a random selection process (or so we were told.) Therefore, there was no reason to put blood over our doors as the ancient Hebrews had done on the first Passover.

I watched one night as they led a young Cheyenne away in shackles. He had never gotten in trouble, worked every day, volunteered for several organizations on the yard—in short, he had every reason to ask "Why me?"

As he walked out, slowly, proudly, head held high, looking straight ahead, I remember wondering if he'd prayed not to be taken and realized that, whatever he had prayed, he'd been given strength and grace.

I Will: Proclaim

# Forward Day by Day

✠

*For there is hope for a tree,*
*if it is cut down,*
*that it will sprout again,*
*and its shoots will not cease.*

— JOB 14:7

Not long after I was imprisoned, my dad told me the story of an eastern short-leaf pine that was growing up through a rock not far from his house. There was no visible sustenance for this little pine tree—just bare, moss-covered sandstone—and, yet, there it was, sprouting away.

Dad went on to tell me that I would do well to imitate that little tree, to grow where I was, despite the apparent lack of conventional nourishment. Of course, like most good advice I received in those days, it went over my head. That didn't stop my dad from giving me regular reports on "the little pine."

Right out of that half-ton rock, it continued to grow. One foot. Three feet. "Son, it's as tall as I am now." But for me, "the little pine" was just a quaint story my dad repeated, probably to keep his spirits up. I could envision a tree growing out of a rock, but I couldn't feel the connection.

That is, not until I got out of prison and stood under the twelve-foot pine and looked down where it had broken the rock as it grew.

# Master of the Universe

*Seeking God Day by Day, 2013*

⁜

*At bottom, the whole concern of religion is with the manner*
*of our acceptance of the universe.*
— WILLIAM JAMES

This spring has been wet. After being in a moderate-to-severe drought for several years and struggling to help keep green things growing, it's a piece of good fortune to hear thunder and rain and see four inches in our rain gauge.

Last summer didn't get especially hot, but there was literally no rain for months. Hundred-year-old trees died. Everything was brown. Wildfires raged. Animals foraged for food and water. Almost everything we tried to grow died.

The year before there was a little rain but then it got hot. Temperatures of 100-plus reigned throughout the summer. Almost everything we tried to grow died.

Yesterday I was mowing, and the grass was as thick and luscious as a carpet! I don't believe I've ever seen grass that rich, certainly not in our yard. And, thing is, it was in the same area that had been brown the years before.

Before long I was congratulating myself on how well I had done in making this grass grow. Full of pride, I'm pretty sure I was grinning as I mowed. Then it dawned on me that I'd not done anything different this year from the previous several years; the only thing different was the amount of rain.

After that I was still grinning, but now it was at my arrogance and amnesia because I had forgotten once again who was in charge of the universe.

# Forward Day by Day

*Tuesday, February 18, 2014*

✠

*Be joyful in the LORD, all you lands.*
— PSALM 100:1A

And what, exactly, does that joyful noise sound like?

Depending on the person, it can range anywhere from an encompassing chorus of cicadas and tree frogs that animates the spring and summer night to the roar of high-performance engines as they race by the stands at a NASCAR event. Some good ol' hand-clappin', foot-stompin', soulful choir-singing spirituals, the pulsating purr of a cat, the rush of wind as it blows through the car window on a beautiful day. A baby's laugh, the rendition of a much-loved classical piece played on an old Victrola, and the sounds of pounding basketballs and squeaking rubber on gym floors. The still, white silence of new snow, the womblike rush of ocean waves caressing the shore, and the guttural throb of a Harley, and any number of the myriad sounds of Creation.

It's not whether we agree on what the sound is—it's whether we make it, listen to it, experience it, and then, in the name of peace, allow others the freedom to do the same.

# Forward Day by Day

*Tuesday, February 25, 2014*

✠

*The beginning of wisdom is this:*
*Get wisdom, and whatever else you get, get insight.*
— Proverbs 4:7

Some thirty-five years ago, when I was a teenager and beginning to stray from the way I'd been raised, my grandpa would grin when I stumbled and say I'd better do something different. He had lived a life of sobriety the whole time I'd been alive, and when he suggested I try Alcoholics Anonymous, I would smile and tell him I'd think about it.

Truth was, I was glad AA was there for old drunks like him—my whole life I'd heard he used to be the town drunk—but I was just a kid who liked to have some fun and party. My only problem, I thought, was people wouldn't leave me alone and let me do what I wanted to do—and when I wanted to do it.

My grandpa died before I got my life together. I like to imagine him being pleased with the way it's turned out and nodding every once and a while when I do something right. And I sure hope he knows how lucky I was to have his wise counsel and how, after his death, that wisdom finally sank in and continues to light my path today.

I Will: Proclaim

# CHAPTER 4

# Seek and Serve

*Will you seek and serve Christ in all persons,*
*loving your neighbor as yourself?*

## I will, with God's help.

# God's Upside-downedness

*Release: Meditations from Prison, Day 9, 1995*

✠

*The people will come from east and west,*
*from north and south,*
*and will eat in the kingdom of God.*
*Indeed, some are last who will be first,*
*and some are first who will be last.*
— LUKE 13:29-30

This verse has a special appeal to me. Knowing my situation, I'm sure you can appreciate why. Being shut away from the rest of society, I feel like I'm "last."

Beyond that, beyond my hurt feelings, lies a magnificent truth, a monumental happening. All across the United States and the world, the Holy Spirit is moving in prisons and other institutions. I see it here, and I know that it's happening all over. The dregs of society are inheriting God's promise.

A friend of mine—once an incurable drunk, mental hospital patient, homeless man, now a recovering alcoholic, man of God, college professor—looked me in the eye and told me that the great spiritual leaders of the twenty-first century are being prepared right now. Being prepared, he said, in our prisons and institutions.

We shouldn't be too hasty to discount a person based on society's measuring stick. Jesus tells us he is using a different ruler to see how we measure up.

Lord, I am hungry; feed me in your kingdom.

# Doing Good—For Whom?

*Release: Meditations from Prison, Day 21, 1995*

⁜

*So you also, when you have done all that you*
*were ordered to do,*
*say, "We are worthless slaves;*
*we have done only what we ought to have done!"*
— LUKE 17:10

When I was a child, I wanted to be rewarded for everything I did that was good. I don't think I was unlike most other children. We all want to be told we're doing a good job. We want a pat on the back. I, however, kept this attitude. It was especially prevalent during my adolescence and early adult years. It got so bad that I would do good things just to hear someone tell me how good I was!

I think this is what Jesus was talking about. He knew that once we get caught up in the ego gratification of doing good, our egos take over our hearts and corrupt any good, any pure deed.

Doing good deeds in secret is one way to keep the ego from being one of the motivations of good works. Still, I can get wrapped up in patting myself on the back for all the good I'm doing for God. I've really got to work at this.

I've got to look at doing good in three different ways. It's something I get to do as a Christian. It's something I want to do as a Christian. It's something I've got to do as a Christian.

I Will: Seek and Serve

# Deciding When

*Release: Meditations from Prison, Day 27, 1995*

✠

*My friends, if anyone is detected in a transgression,*
*you who have received the Spirit should restore*
*such a one in a spirit of gentleness...*
*Bear one another's burdens,*
*and in this way you will fulfill the law of Christ.*
— GALATIANS 6:1A, 2

Prison, for the most part, is segregated. It's either by race, religion, or the lack thereof. So, what would Paul say to me about bearing another's burdens—if that other were "different"?

I struggle with that question. First of all, prison is not a place to stick your nose into other people's business. It can get you killed. Second, some people don't want "Christian" advice. Third, some people don't want "Caucasian" advice. Fourth, some people don't want "Episcopalian" advice. I could go on and on.

Paul talks of a "spirit of gentleness." I must be extremely gentle when expressing my opinion to others. Taking a passive role is not always the easy thing to do—especially when I think I have the right way—but Jesus' way isn't always easy. Being gentle helps people to accept what I'm offering.

So when do I get involved? Well, as Paul says, "So then, whenever we have an opportunity, let us work for the good of all."

Lord, give us wisdom to know when to speak and when to be silent.

# Forward Day by Day

*Monday, March 23, 1998*

✠

*Do not seek your own advantage, but that of the other.*
— I CORINTHIANS 10:24

Back in the late '30s, hopeless drunks were just that. Hopeless. Sanitariums and graveyards were the cure. What happened? A couple of drunks tapped into an age-old spiritual truth. It's at the top of this page.

Before Alcoholics Anonymous had a name, one of its very first members was practicing this truth. He was hosting AA meetings in a motel room. However, things weren't going that well.

"I've been there every night, made coffee, bought donuts, done everything I can think to do, and it's not working. I've really tried, but not a one of those men has stayed sober. This just won't work," he said.

"Oh, honey, it does work. You've stayed sober," his wife replied.

It all started with someone caring about someone else. Then, someone else caring about someone else. Sixty years later, from that very shaky and improbable beginning, there emerged a fellowship of recovering alcoholics, numbering in the millions.

Do you know what's so beautiful about this age-old spiritual truth?

It's not just for drunks. Just like all spiritual truths, it's an equal opportunity employer—it's for everybody.

Apply today. The pay's good.

I Will: Seek and Serve

# Forward Day by Day

*Wednesday, April 1, 1998*

✛

*Truly I tell you,*
*whoever does not receive*
*the kingdom of God as a little child*
*will never enter it.*
— MARK 10:15

"Pwaise tha Lawd!" He's subject to stand up and yell it at anytime. It's not that noticeable during, say, a Pentecostal or Baptist service. But, man, let him cut loose during a somber Episcopal service, and it'll raise a few heads. He doesn't stop there. We occasionally have speakers. Bands, too. If the mood strikes him, he'll yell it whenever.

I'm envious. For Jimmy, the kingdom is at hand. Look into his eyes and the look of joy there leaves no doubt as to his proximity to the kingdom. I sometimes wonder if he's an angel.

He went up for parole recently. I saw him the next day. His usually bright spirit was dark.

"Bo, they turned me down fo pawole," he said. I knew they had, because in Oklahoma, they turn down everyone. It doesn't matter what you've done to change, they're doing their best to keep everyone in prison as long as possible. There's no reason to it, and I struggled to explain this to Jimmy in a way he'd understand.

Finally, failing miserably at finding the right words, I asked him if he wanted to get an ice cream. My treat.

"Pwaise tha Lawd!" he said, and it was then that I knew he'd found the words to cope with our situation.

---

# Forward Day by Day

*Wednesday in Holy Week, April 8, 1998*

✚

*I give you a new command, that you love one another.*
— JOHN 13:34A

Read it. Only eleven words. So simple. So complex. So uncomplicated. So multi-dimensional. So easy sounding. So hard to do. So shallow. So deep.

Once again, Jesus' message is extremely paradoxical. Not the message itself, but the reality of the message. Taken at face value, it sounds really plain. Really easy.

We think of our grandchildren, our grandparents, our wives, our husbands, our girlfriends, our boyfriends, our best friends, our sons, our daughters, our dads, our moms. It's simple to see; love is the answer. What would we do without those we love? With them in mind, Jesus' command sounds really easy, and we find ourselves saying, "I can follow this command. It's an easy one."

Then, we step off our front porch, and we're confronted with all the people we don't want to love, from the person who cut us off in traffic yesterday to that one person we swore we'd never forgive. Every single person who has ever done us wrong. People we don't understand. Homeless people. Street people. Evil people. Mean people. People who scare us. The worst. Saddam Hussein and Jeffrey Dahmer.

It turns our comfortable world upside-down, doesn't it? That's a pretty good sign Jesus has his hand in it.

I Will: Seek and Serve

# Forward Day by Day

*Wednesday, April 29, 1998*

✣

*My friends and companions draw back from my affliction;*
*my neighbors stand afar off.*
— PSALM 38:11

A few weeks ago, I was speaking to a local high school tour group. Most of the morning had been spent dispelling myths and stereotypes. After the students got over bald-headed, muscled-up, tattooed guys named Bubba, we began a very useful and enlightening dialogue. As it always does, a familiar question then found its way into the conversation.

We'd spent the morning out on the compound, and thanks to the prisoners who take care of the flora around here and put their souls into their work, it looks nice in the spring. The question came from an attractive young lady with bright eyes. She wanted to know if we really thought we were being punished.

I didn't know what to say. I wanted to tell her how hard even this "nice" prison had been, so I struggled to come up with the single most "punishing" factor of the past eleven years. And, that's when it hit me.

"What hurts is that every day I get up and, at least one time a day, realize that you guys don't want me around you any more," I told her. I think she understood.

I used to be like that girl. I used to think prisoners were "others." I had a lot of opinions.

I was wrong.

---

# The Salvage Man

*God Is Not In the Thesaurus:*
*Stories from an Oklahoma Prison, 1999*

⁜

*The stone that the builders rejected*
*has become the cornerstone.*
— MATTHEW 21:42

I t was no different from other mornings in prison. The prisoner woke up, looked at his clock—6:45—and at his still-sleeping cell partner. He lay there a minute, rolled over on his stomach, raised himself to his knees, and, still in bed said a short prayer: Dear God, whatever. Thank You.

He got up, made a cup of instant coffee, walked out on the run, and lit a cigarette. He'd started smoking again, and while it bothered him, he inhaled deeply and enjoyed it. Reaching into the pocket of his gym shorts, he pulled out his daily meditation booklet. As he'd been doing for a good while, he began reading someone else's words on life. Considering the mess he'd made of his, doing it his way, he figured it didn't hurt to accept some guidance.

When his blurry vision stumbled across the word salvation, he saw salvage. He went back to the first of the sentence and read it again. It plainly said salvation, right there in black and white. Why, then, was he still seeing salvage?

The first thing that came to mind was Skeeter McAlroy, the old man who'd run the junkyard in his small town. He could see him, plain as day, standing there in his grease-stained coveralls, absentmindedly chewing on a huge wad of tobacco as its brown juice ran a crooked line from the corner of his mouth down through his old, white beard.

He smiled at himself. It was like him to make these seemingly unrelated jumps between scripture and life. Ever since he'd begun writing, his mom had told him that he was going to have a hard time understanding the Bible because he placed too much importance on language, believing that words had dual meanings and thinking that when something says this, it really means that. She believed that the words in the Bible were simple and sacred and her son's wordsmithing complicated plain instructions and risked the chance of corrupting these mandates. He didn't think so.

He figured that God was the master poet and enjoyed the complexity of language as much as anyone, and he'd long ago decided that God was a lot smarter than he could ever hope to comprehend. Trying to fit God into a human-sized box was silly. And if Jesus could speak in parables, why couldn't he play with words and search to uncover meanings beneath the obvious?

And so he thought of the way that Skeeter had run that junkyard. Skeeter didn't conform to society's standards, beginning with the way he wore his tobacco juice and the way he dressed. Except for the time he saw him at grandpa's funeral, he'd never seen Skeeter in anything but baggy, grease-stained coveralls. Skeeter mumbled when he talked, partly because of the wad in his mouth, partly because he talked to himself. Skeeter was definitely an oddball and walked to a different beat.

Not only did Skeeter look and act differently, his occupation was a deviation from the norm. He took pride in restoring to beauty what someone else had thrown away. He could even make things better than new. He'd dig through the piles at the city dump, rummaging for worthy objects. How did he choose? What did he look for while he sifted through garbage? Was it a glint of light off an old, tarnished lamp? Was it the way the pull cord dangled from the long-dead motor of a rusty lawnmower? Was it the absence of food in an abandoned refrigerator or the lonely sound of its broken door blown back and forth by an occasional breeze? What was it?

Could Skeeter see the personality in the old oak dresser peeking through layers of peeling paint? Were the giggles of a former owner still ringing from the broken bell dangling from the bicycle with no wheels and a rotting seat? Was that it?

Maybe it was all that and maybe it wasn't. Maybe every piece of worthless junk that Skeeter ever laid his magical eyes on became a potential masterpiece, a work of art. Maybe in the twinkling blue eyes that sat above that dirty beard and mumbling mouth, nothing was beyond repair.

The prisoner blew out a puff of smoke, and, leaving one foot in scripture and setting the other one down in real life, he decided that God probably looked a lot like Skeeter. As far as he could see, they had a lot in common.

That gave the prisoner a sense of hope. He'd spent the last thirteen years in one of society's junkyards. For all intents and purposes, he'd been thrown away. But that was okay, for if he had not been thrown away, he would never have known what it was to be salvaged. He knew exactly what those forgotten pieces of junk felt like when Skeeter's gaze settled on them.

He smiled again and told God, and Skeeter, thank you.

# Forward Day by Day

✠

*Someone asked him,*
*"Lord, will only a few be saved?"*
— LUKE 13:23

Apparently, much like they still do today, the people of Jesus' day were overly concerned about everyone else's salvation.

This piece of scripture has been used as a shield for elitist, separatist, exclusionist sects of people who like to claim they're the only real Christians. If you don't believe exactly like them, you're going to hell where there'll be "weeping" and "gnashing of teeth."

Not only does this scare tactic turn following Jesus into a lesser-of-two-evils kind of choice, it misses the point of Jesus' parable entirely.

Jesus isn't saying that only a few people are "cut out to be Christians." Think about it. Why would the guy who hung out with freaks and geeks suddenly switch gears and make up a VIP list for an exclusive country club in the clouds?

What if the carpenter is simply saying it's hard, doing what's right? It's difficult, walking in love? It's easier following your stomach compared to following your heart? The pain that comes from living out of self is hell—a weeping and gnashing-of-the teeth affair? If you try his way, you'll see it can be heaven?

For those who still insist on a guest list, he offers the following: "Indeed, some are last who will be first, and some are first who will be last" (Luke 13:30).

# Forward Day by Day

*Saturday, March 24, 2001*

✠

*May the graciousness of the LORD our God be upon us,*
*prosper the work of our hands;*
*prosper our handiwork.*
— PSALM 90:17

In addition to writing, the work of my hands is either dragging brush or picking up other people's discarded garbage. The crew I belong to works along state highways where we either clear right-of-ways of brush and trees or march along the sides of the road and stab trash with sticks. It's beyond menial labor. It's a modern-day chain gang. We have INMATE stenciled across the back of our blue shirts and DayGlo-orange mesh vests. We're surrounded by armed guards on four-wheel ATVs.

It'd be real easy to become disgusted at this brow-mopping labor, much less this manner of social tattooing. After all, it's the twenty-first century.

And, yet, believe it or not, I don't mind. I did at first, but that was before that day last summer, smack dab in the middle of one of those infamous, Oklahoma 107-degree days. We'd been walking forever; my shirt was plastered to my torso with sweat.

I was in the middle of this thought: "I don't deserve this. I'm not gonna keep doing this for these people." That was when God asked me if I'd do it for him instead.

Who are you working for?

# Forward Day by Day

*Friday, May 3, 2002*

✠

*When you reap the harvest of your land,*
*you shall not reap to the very edges of your field,*
*or gather the gleanings of your harvest;*
*you shall leave them for the poor and for the alien.*
— LEVITICUS 23:22

It was the night of the Orange Bowl, and the Oklahoma Sooners were in the process of winning the 2000 National Championship. In Oklahoma, not unlike some other states, football is religion. Those of us in prison were as devoted as anyone. We were having a party.

A bunch of us had chipped in and brought a spread worthy of praise, especially considering prison limitations. By kickoff, we were settled in front of the TV.

One of our friends couldn't make the gathering, so we made him a plate, and I carried it to his cell. On the way, a young man sitting in the prison day room noticed the pile of chips, meat, tomatoes, onions, jalapenos, refried beans, black olives, melted cheese, and sour cream piled atop the plate in my hands.

"Man, that sure looks good," he said.

"It is," I replied and hurried on to deliver the tray and get back to the game.

See? I get it wrong more often than I get it right. I should have invited the young man. The rules are plain: care more for others than I do for myself. I can't follow them, and, yet, the light shines on. How do I explain that? I don't. I can't. I am unworthy.

# Forward Day by Day

*Wednesday, May 15, 2002*

⊕

*Then the whole town came out to meet Jesus;*
*and when they saw him,*
*they begged him to leave their neighborhood.*
— MATTHEW 8:34

I beg him to leave all the time. Today a guy stuck his laundry in the dryer ahead of mine when mine had been sitting there first. Once it was clear to me what happened, out came his laundry and in went mine. You just don't do that, or put up with it, in prison. So when I couldn't learn who the line jumper was I left a nasty note on the dryer, daring him to touch my clothes.

Boy, that's real Christlike, isn't it? It's a daily thing. My rights, my needs will supersede another's, and, wham, out of the neighborhood goes Jesus.

It's a scary proposition, following Jesus. Remember, this radical made his contemporaries so mad they killed him. I don't know why his causing the hogs to jump off the cliff made everyone so mad but apparently it did. Maybe they were planning something with the money that could be made from the hogs. Or maybe what they saw frightened them to the core.

Jesus is cool when we're loving people who don't put their clothes ahead of us in the laundry. Thing is, Jesus asks us to love those who upset the status quo. Then, we ask him to leave the neighborhood.

I Will: Seek and Serve

# Forward Day by Day

*Sunday, May 19, 2002 — Day of Pentecost*

✠

*If you forgive the sins of any, they are forgiven them;*
*if you retain the sins of any, they are retained.*
— JOHN 20:23

Resentment kills. Resenting another person is like taking poison and waiting for that person to die. Resentment is like acid; it eats up the container it's in.

Remember, we started these three months searching for the light. Resentment cannot thrive in the light.

If your light is the street lamp that burns on your comfortable street, resentment is the vandal's rock, thrown with meanness that plunges your safe neighborhood into long scary shadows and eerie unknown noises.

If your light is the sun on a perfect May day, resentment is the bruised, blue-steel thunderhead that comes rolling in from the southwest, bringing hail, strong winds, and darkness at three in the afternoon.

If your light is a crude, tallow candle burning a hole in the pitch-black night, resentment is the pair of fingers that pinches out the flame with a "phhsst." If your light is the smile on your face, resentment is the dark scowl.

If your light is Jesus, resentment is the pounding hammer that drove the nails into his hands, the agony of hanging like that and, finally, the darkness of blood running into his eyes.

Resentment kills.

---

# Forward Day by Day

*Tuesday, June 11, 2002 — Saint Barnabas*

✠

*The kingdom of heaven has come near.*
—MATTHEW 10:7B

This is one of the ways I know I'm a Christian. The kingdom of heaven is not a carrot-on-a-stick reward. I don't believe in and worship God and try to follow Jesus' example because the kingdom of heaven is where I'll go when I die. I believe in and worship God and try to follow Jesus' example because, when I'm able to, the kingdom of heaven happens. Right here and right now.

Knowing the kingdom of heaven has come near, and knowing that if it can take root in me it can blossom in anyone, helps me to get glimpses of it. Last week, after a particularly hot, humid day on the work crew, I was given just such a gift. I'd been irritable all day—up to my neck in poison ivy—but also because, sometimes, I'm simply oversensitive and judgmental.

I can't tell you if it came in through my barred window and melted its way into my heart or if it was already there, but suddenly the kingdom was near. It was inside me. Likewise, it was inside the armed robbers in front of me and the drug smuggler beside. It was inside the men I liked and the ones who got on my nerves. It was even inside the armed guard who abuses his authority.

The kingdom of heaven can show up and flourish anywhere; be on the lookout.

I Will: Seek and Serve

# Forward Day by Day

*Sunday, July 28, 2002 — 10 Pentecost*

✥

*God said to him, "Because you have asked this,*
*and have not asked for yourself…"*
— 1 KINGS 3:11

Gary is nineteen years older than me. We've been running together for a decade. He's taught me a lot about God. If it's not walking his ninety-something year-old mother around the visiting room, or dancing with nursing home residents at a regular cookout some of the prisoners host for an area nursing home, then it's his refusal to talk bad about anyone and the way he encourages every single runner I've ever seen him run by. If it's none of these, it's the way he feeds the sparrows.

A few days ago, we were preparing to run when a sparrow came hopping up to Gary. Not to within a few feet—I mean it came right up to him.

"Hey, little fella," he said. "You better get off the track, someone's liable to run over you. C'mon." He began to shoo the friendly bird off the track. Every time he'd get it out of the way and return to the track, it would follow him, hopping right up under his feet.

"C'mon, little fella. You can't hop around out here. Someone will hurt you." He tried to herd it to the grass again.

"Gary, I think that little bird recognizes you from a time you've fed it," I said.

"Nah, it's just friendly."

My friend refuses to take credit for a lot. He puts himself last a lot. I learn a lot.

# In Transition

*Wednesday, March 17, 2004*

✠

*I judge no one.*
— JOHN 8:15B

Jesus said that. When is the last time you heard a sermon on John 8:15? Ever seen "John 8:15" sticking up out of the end zone stands as they are about to kick an extra point on *Monday Night Football*? Why, I want to know, is this not as broadly publicized as being a part of Christianity as are other scriptures?

I work with a young lady who no longer attends church. She says she is tired of going and feeling guiltier when she leaves than when she got there. She is a wonderfully bright and good-hearted person who treats every person she meets with dignity and respect. Day in and day out, she shines with that glow that I attribute to only one Source. And yet she hasn't found a church that can help her to feel better when the service is over, as opposed to worse.

I am sure you know someone like that. I battle everyday with calling it quits. Daily I question calling myself a Christian and belonging to a group of people that I feel increasingly alienated from.

Why do I feel alienated from what I see as passing for Christianity these days? Too much judgment. Too much anger. Too much guilt.

In the book *Alcoholics Anonymous,* there is a phrase, "attraction rather than promotion." This means that the people who belong to AA do not proselytize. They know AA is not for everyone, not even everyone with a drinking problem. They are okay with that. They take the people who want to be there and do what people in AA do, and that is it. Inevitably, their lives get better, and the miracle that is recovery begins to shine through them.

Sure, people in AA have their flaws just like everyone else, and I am sure there is a fair amount of character assassination that takes place in meeting halls across the world. The spirit of AA is "never to show intolerance or hatred toward drinking as an institution" because "a spirit of intolerance might repel alcoholics whose lives could have been saved had it not been for such stupidity" (*Alcoholics Anonymous*, page 103). Recovering alcoholics worldwide save lives every day by not doing anything other than living their own lives to the best of their ability and letting others come of their own free will.

Christianity could learn from such an example. We would do well to be able to say that we were careful never to show intolerance or hatred toward people who do not necessarily believe like us, for such an attitude might repel a child of God whose life otherwise could have been saved or, at the very least, enriched.

Right before he said the part about not judging, Jesus said, "I am the light of the world. Whoever follows me will never walk in darkness but will have the light of life."

Jesus simply says, "Follow me, and you'll experience an existence you never dreamed of."

He didn't say, "Follow me, or else." I think it is time we quit saying it.

# In Transition

*Monday, March 29, 2004*

✛

*Has the potter no right over the clay,*
*to make out of the same lump*
*one object for special use and another for ordinary use?*
— ROMANS 9:21

My five closest friends in the whole world (excluding Debb, my wife, who also counts these men among her closest friends) are doing life sentences for first-degree murder. Same as I was.

I miss them terribly, and it is hard to make new friends. First of all it takes time, and second of all, there is nothing wrong with my old ones—except that I cannot see them because they can't get out. Or, at least, haven't gotten out yet.

Day in and day out, I wonder why. Why am I sitting here right now and they are in there? Every time I eat a meal, I wonder what they would think about the delicious spread in front of me. Every Friday for seventeen years, I ate a breaded fish patty. Every Tuesday, pancakes for breakfast. Wednesday it was usually beans. Now, on any day of the week, I can eat Chinese, Mexican, Italian, or whatever. Just about every morning, as I get dressed for work and am going over my clothes, wondering what I will wear, I think about them and their limited choices: what will it be today: gray or gray? Don't get me wrong; I am not all of sudden saying that things, whether they are tastier food or nicer clothes, are what matter. All I am saying is that I am having trouble accepting all this while they are still in there.

You see, I am no more deserving than any one of them. Yet, here I am, and there they are. Four of them have been in longer than I was—

anywhere from eighteen to thirty-five years—and one has been in only sixteen years. (It's staggering to consider that he came in when he was sixteen years old. To have spent half of one's entire life locked up…The friend with thirty-five years came in when he was eighteen. That was in 1968. He is fifty-something now, and he passed the halfway mark a long time ago.)

Yes, they killed someone. Yes, when you open their file, it says, "First-Degree Murder." So did mine. In fact, I got an idea of how terrible that looks on paper when I filled out the application for my current job. Maybe I had gotten used to seeing it in prison because I do not remember ever having the reaction I had when I saw my hand write it on that piece of paper. I was terrified to turn it in.

At the same time, the things I know about these men you cannot put in a file. Never mind the fact that each and every one of them had a direct bearing on the fact that I was able to turn my life around. Each of these men, at one point or another, was paramount in my being able to scratch and claw and crawl my way back out of the dark. Not only were they paramount at one point or another, they continued to be and are today.

Simply put, I wouldn't be here today, and you would not be reading these words today if it were not for these men.

Gosh, I'm so grateful. At the same time, without them, this all feels wrong.

# Who Is Jesus?

*Praying Day by Day, 2009*

✠

*But who do you say that I am?*
— MARK 8:29

Brother Ron Fender, a member of the Episcopal Brotherhood of Saint Gregory, saw Jesus one day. He wasn't "Brother Ron" yet, just Ron. If I remember the story correctly, he was doing his graduate work at Harvard when, walking across the campus one day, he happened to notice a homeless man digging through the trash for something to eat. Their eyes met and in that homeless man Ron said he saw his Lord rummaging for scraps. Right then he knew he was going to become part of a solution to help homeless people, as opposed to part of a system that regularly has folks—possibly Jesus himself—eating out of trash cans.

Not long after that, Ron began a ministry in which he cares for the feet of the homeless. In the beginning it was just Ron, some soap, and a bucket. Today that ministry includes a podiatrist and several nursing students.

You might think it would be difficult to be in the same room with Ron. After all, how could he not have the attitude of "what are you doing for Jesus?" Yet it's nothing like that. He's gracious and unassuming when it comes to discussing what one does with one's beliefs and, in the very end, service to others seems to stand silently as a sort of benchmark.

Still, if I fall prey to comparison, I find myself sorely lacking. It seems, most often, I am more consumed with who I am than with anything else, and Jesus will have to dig through a few more trash cans while I attend to my well-being.

# Forward Day by Day

*Saturday, April 2, 2011*

✢

*So they picked up stones to throw at him,*
*but Jesus hid himself and went out of the temple.*
— JOHN 8:59

In many ways the Judaism of Jesus' day is akin to today's Christianity: it was considered by Jews to be the preferred way. Religion in Jesus' day was all about who was clean and who was unclean; today it is sometimes about who is saved and who is unsaved.

And then comes Jesus, this totally unqualified person, saying basically that there is no front and back of the line; in fact, there is no line. It is no understatement to say that Jesus was outside their box.

Imagine what a shock it would be today to encounter some young, uneducated, maybe scruffy, definitely alternative, let's say, woman, with a skin color different from yours walking into your church and saying with calm confidence that what she sees there is a far cry from what her heart tells her when she reads God's word or when she hears answers to her prayers.

Yes, you'd pick up your stones, real stones, emotional stones, word stones, mental stones—no matter, stones nonetheless—and you'd throw them.

Do we want to be the ones who drive Jesus away?

# Forward Day by Day

*Sunday, April 10, 2011 — 5 Lent*

✛

*Lord, if you had been here, my brother would not have died.*
— JOHN 11:21

As you're reading this, I will be approaching the eight-year mark since I got out of prison. I can look back over that time and fondly recall men who were there for me and to whom I owe my life.

Rodney wore pink shorts and played the flute. In prison, that's a hard feat to pull off and still maintain your boundaries and not be preyed upon. He taught me much about the real essence of manhood.

Several years ago, Rodney was diagnosed with cancer. He called me once in the midst of his long and painful (and ultimately unsuccessful) treatment. I could hear the pain and weariness in his voice while he told me how grateful he was to have lived the life he had lived and how hopeful he was to navigate this portion of it with grace.

"Man, Rod," I commented, "here I am out here, not being grateful for every single thing I have, and there you are, going through this with such courage and character. Man, dude, you're the warrior."

"Oh, brother," he replied, "we're on the same journey, just riding different horses."

I Will: Seek and Serve

# Forward Day by Day

*Friday, April 22, 2011 — Good Friday*

✠

*The woman said to Peter,
"You are not also one of this man's disciples, are you?"
He said, "I am not."*
— JOHN 18:17

I had just gotten a promotion and an office. Sitting in the office on my very first morning, I looked at the barc walls, not believing my good fortune and fearing I was in over my head.

Then I heard a heated exchange outside my closed door. One of the voices belonged to a senior staff member whom everyone revered. It was a volatile exchange and both parties spoke inappropriately.

Later, in the staff meeting, I listened as the staff member told his version. He said the client had attacked him and, with a trembling voice, that all of us would be in danger if this violent person were allowed to stay.

I wanted to speak up and say it wasn't exactly as it was being told. Yes, the client had reacted in anger, but the dialogue had begun in an assaulting manner, and they had both reacted in kind—I'd heard the whole thing, and knew it was nothing like what was being reported!

The resulting crescendo of consensus in favor of the staff member left me afraid to speak. They kicked a young lady out of treatment as I hung my head and remained quiet.

# Forward Day by Day

*Thursday, February 13, 2014*

✣

*And you will know the truth, and the truth will make you free.*
— John 8:32

The man across from me had a .357 Magnum in his mouth two days before our conversation. Events in his life had piled up, one after another, until he could see no other way out from the pain and hopelessness of his existence. Most of the events weren't even major stressors but, stacked end on end, they resembled a mountain he didn't think he could ever cross.

Thankfully, before he mustered the courage or desperation or both to pull the trigger, his little dog jumped up on his lap and began licking his arm and wagging her tail.

As he kept talking with me, he seemed to be trying to lead up to a confession of sorts. He'd pause, say, "I've never told anyone this," then falter and change the subject. As his story unfolded, he sounded a lot more like an everyday Joe than a suicidal John Doe.

Finally, he seemed to be ready and began again.

"I know I'm a grown man and so I shouldn't say this, but…" He stalled.

"I'm so afraid."

Tears flowed, and, with each tear, he began to look more and more hopeful.

I Will: Seek and Serve

# Forward Day by Day

*Thursday, February 20, 2014*

✠

*If you know that he is righteous,*
*you may be sure that everyone who does right has been born of him.*
— 1 JOHN 2:29

I was still in prison the first time I saw him. He was standing in a flower garden, digging and talking to anyone who stopped. He was quite a sight: long, wild, brown hair streaked with gray and an unruly, scraggly beard to match. I used to think that John the Baptist probably looked something like Jeff.

The next time I saw him, he was the lone white face in a roomful of Muslim brothers, kneeling in prayer. He also attended the Episcopal service on Sunday evenings. One day I asked him why he was a Muslim. "Muslim literally means one who surrenders, Bo. You're a Muslim, too, on your good days."

We became good friends. When I got out, we stayed in touch, and when Jeff got out a year or so after me, he became a regular fixture in our household. Debb loved him; our pets loved him. The plants certainly loved him.

He was one of the gentlest men I've ever known, and I can't wrap my mind or my heart around a religion that would exclude his righteousness, either here on earth or in the hereafter.

# CHAPTER 5

# Strive for Justice

*Will you strive for justice
and peace among all people,
and respect the dignity
of every human being?*

I will, with God's help.

# Hard Decisions

*Release: Meditations from Prison, Day 6, 1995*

✠

*Do you think that I have come to bring peace to the earth?*
*No, I tell you, but rather division!*
*From now on five in one household will be divided,*
*three against two and two against three.*
— LUKE 12:51-52

This line of thought has always bothered me. I prefer to bask in the warm, pleasant glow of God's Peace—the Peace which passes all understanding—rather than face the unpleasantness of division.

But the truth is there is division. If you've ever found yourself debating whether to concur with a friend or go with God's voice, ask your conscience. Then you understand what it is to be divided.

Jesus is telling us that if we decide to follow him, we are going to face conflicts. We are going to discover that his way is not necessarily easy. He's telling us that sometimes if we follow him, we will be divided against friends and families.

Jesus' earthly ministry went against "the way things were" in his day. Yes, the One who teaches us all about peace, love, and joy faced a lot of division. God, please grant us the strength to imitate your Son, our Savior.

Lord, grant us your peace.

# Tom's Wisdom

*Release: Meditations from Prison, Day 18, 1995*

✠

*Mercy triumphs over judgment.*
— James 2:13b

Tom, my old cell-partner, and I were at the University of Oklahoma speaking to a class of sociology students. For the better part of the class, they had asked interesting questions about our lives in prison. What was it like to be addicted to drugs and feel as if you had no control over your life? What was it like to learn, as an adult in prison, things that most of us learn as teenagers? Isn't it hard on your family? What was it like to realize that, even though you've made quality changes and straightened your lives up, you may not get out of prison?

All in all, it had been a rewarding experience for all of us. Suddenly, an angry young woman spoke up and said that we had it too easy, that we were there to be punished, not helped.

I struggled for an answer. For eight years, I'd been locked up in an over-sized dog pen, stuck out in the woods where society didn't have to look at me. Couldn't she see that I was being punished? I was so frustrated at her venomous response. I was getting ready to tell her what I thought of her self-righteous attitude.

Just then, Tom whispered to me, "Mercy triumphs over judgment."

Amen, Tom.

# Forward Day by Day

*Tuesday, March 3, 1998*

✠

*God chose what is low and despised in the world,*
*things that are not, to reduce to nothing things that are.*
— 1 CORINTHIANS 1:28

He did. He chose some pretty dubious characters to spread his message. Slaves, prisoners, crazies, a long-haired, locust-eating, wild man, and a gang of roguish fishermen led by a radical, extremely left-wing carpenter. Being a long-haired, little bit crazy, radical prisoner, I feel at home among that crowd.

A couple of years ago, I wrote a series of these meditations. Before I began, I was worried that people would shut me out—despise me because I was lowly—and miss the message. They didn't. Far from it. They carried a very powerful message back to me. So, again, I ask; please don't shut out the message.

I know. On the surface, it doesn't make sense that God would use such unlikely people to carry this most important message.

But when I realize what the message is, it dawns on me that no one would know more about it than those in dire need of it. The experts. It makes perfect sense when you consider the message.

The message? Love.

The messenger? You.

You're in good company.

# The House That Jack Built

*God Is Not In the Thesaurus:*
*Stories from an Oklahoma Prison, 1999*

⊹

*"But woe to you Pharisees...[you] neglect justice and the love of God...*
*Woe also to you lawyers, because you load people down with burdens hard*
*to bear, and you yourselves do not lift a finger to ease them...*
*Woe to you lawyers! For you have taken away the key of knowledge..."*
*When he went outside, the scribes and the Pharisees*
*began to be very hostile toward him.*
— LUKE 11:42, 46, 52, 53

A guy can't have too many heroes. Michael Jordan comes to mind; he's such an inspiration to millions of young people. When I was a kid, my heroes were my dad, Mohammed Ali, and Dr. J. There was also a time when my heroes were people who pushed the constraints of acceptability; there's still a soft spot in my heart for Jimi Hendrix, Jim Morrison, and Janis Joplin. Now I've added some new heroes—John the Baptist, Jesus, Martin Luther King Jr., Gandhi, and Neil Young. That common denominator—radical—is still present. Radical is defined as "departing sharply from the traditional or usual," and when that tradition becomes oppressive and self-righteous, it takes courage to stand against peer pressure and do the right thing. So, while on one hand it may be surprising to learn that one of my heroes is an ex-prison warden, it is also apropos. That man is Jack Cowley.

I arrived at the Joseph Harp Correctional Center in January 1989 after spending three years at another state prison. Harp, as it was affectionately called, was the talk of the prison system. Over there, it was said, they had a warden who let you get high. They had so many drugs that the guys selling them were having price wars. Open smoke-ins on the ballfield. Conjugal visits once a month. On and on, the rumors were as wild and numerous as the rumor-mongers.

It certainly appealed to me, a young man in search of a better life through the right mixture of chemicals. When I managed to manipulate my transfer to Harp, I was ecstatic. I was finally going to Nirvana. I was moving to Xanadu!

Upon arrival, I was not disappointed. Drugs were plentiful and cheap. It was like one big hippie commune. Unlike other prisons, where the stress was thick, Harp thrived in an atmosphere of peace. There was a huge ballfield with a half-mile track around it. Trees, grass, and flowerbeds abounded, not the red dirt and concrete of other state prisons. Once a month, during summer, we were allowed to have our visits on the ballfield.

Every weekend, during regular visits, our family and friends were allowed to bring in food. Even though the conjugal visits were pure fantasy, Harp was even better than what I had heard.

In most prisons, you're lucky to see the warden once a month. At Harp, I saw the main man two or three times the first week. He was out on the prison yard, talking with the men who lived there. He called people by first names. He laughed. He joked. He'd holler across the yard at someone if he wanted to talk with him. It struck me as strange. Who was this guy?

When other guys talked about the warden, they called him Jack. Not Warden. Not Mister. But Jack. Most of the men were stuck in a limited mindset of addiction and immaturity, and, while they were very thankful that Jack let them get by with so many perks, they viewed the warden as weak for letting us have the things he did. I have to confess to once being a part of that crowd. Sure, I liked it at Harp; it was great, but I did think Jack must be a little touched in the head.

Then I met him.

Once a week, he gave a chalk talk for new arrivals. He told us about a place called the real world. It was a place most of us had forgotten. It was a place where we'd proved we couldn't live. He talked about conventional wisdom and the punitive-based philosophies and other stimulus response fallacies so prevalent in corrections. He even said he knew we thought he was weak for being so nice. He said that was what most of the good old boys who made the laws and ran this state thought too and, were it up to them, we'd be locked in a cell twenty-three hours a day, doing time the way it's seen on TV.

Then he told us about Harp. He believed that if he made this place as much like the real world as possible, then, when we got out, we'd stand an infinitely better chance of being a success, not just a person who'd spent incarceration learning how to do time the old-fashioned way. He told us that he was met with opposition every step of the way, that most lawmakers and their constituents wanted us punished, not catered to, and couldn't see far enough past that fear to understand his philosophy.

He told us that in the local coffee shops when people talked about prison, it wasn't nice. He said the majority of Oklahoma's public wanted us locked up in dark places, scary places, not places with flowers and trees and smiles. They wanted us in real prisons, not the "country club" he was permitting. They wanted us to be sorry we were here, and they figured, unless it was pure misery, we'd never reach that state of penitence.

Jack Cowley took exception. He said the only thing we were going to learn in prisons like that was how to live in prisons like that. And that wasn't going to help us at all when we got out and tried to live in the real world. Even underneath my constant marijuana haze and the double vision of weekly amphetamine use, it made sense.

It took a while, but in that fertile atmosphere I sobered up. Crazy. I'd come to a place where the warden allowed more freedom and more chances for wrong choices, and I started making right choices. Right there in the middle of the land of milk and honey, I decided I was going to have to try and live without milk and honey.

So, I took a scary step into the world of "normal." I wanted to get out as much as the next guy, and it appeared that this place, under Jack's tutelage, was geared toward that end. Not only that, but after I got some sobriety under my belt, it gradually dawned on me that it was actually easier to live without the headaches, heartaches, and other consequences of active addiction.

There's a saying in recovery circles: "Keep coming back...it gets better...then it gets worse...then it gets real...then it gets different... then it gets real different." That pretty much describes the last seven-plus years of my life.

After about two years of sobriety, I was given an early parole hearing. It was a disaster. Murphy's Law was in effect. One parole board member was familiar with the circumstances of my case, and he believed I had received an unusually harsh sentence. He was responsible for my early hearing and assured my family that the board would take a serious look at rectifying the situation. Then a death occurred in his family the week of the hearing, and he was absent. This left me in front of the other four members without their colleague's backing and with no idea why I was there.

I got one vote, from the oldest, most conservative man on the parole board, the hardest vote. Even though I was devastated, I marveled at the fact that this ultra-conservative had voted for me. It was later that I learned he'd contacted Jack and asked him about prisoner number 150656. Jack had spoken up for me.

Later that week, I got a handwritten note in the mail from Jack. (I still carry it in my address book.) It read: Bo, Ain't life a bitch at times? I know that you will be fine. Handling disappointment is what builds character, etc., etc., etc. I know it still hurts. I am sorry for that. Now pick yourself up and show the world that quality of life comes from within. As long as there is a breath in you, there is hope...Don't worry, your folks will be fine too. God bless, JC.

I did manage to pick myself up and, even though I still wanted out, I began to see that the true freedom I'd always been looking for in drugs, and even in release, was inside me. With that spark of truth, I began a new and improved relationship with God. And with Jack Cowley.

This was about the same time that a friend of mine suggested that I write an article for our prison magazine, *Concepts*, and I began to write. Since Jack was directly responsible for the content of our magazine, this involved a working relationship with him. Under his guidance, *Concepts* grew from a stapled, mimeographed flier circulated around the yard into a national award-winning publication boasting a mailing list of over five hundred. *Concepts* writers won state and national awards.

I won a first-place award in the Oklahoma Chapter of The Society of Professional Journalists annual competition, and Jack arranged for me to attend the award banquet. Not only did he allow me to go, I went without the restraints required by the Department of Corrections. It was one of the proudest moments of my life. I felt like a normal person as I sat at my table with a few members of my family and professional journalists from across the state. When they called my name and I walked to the podium to receive my plaque and certificate, I was so grateful, not only because of my success but also because I was being treated like a person.

This success of our magazine brought conflict. The Department of Corrections was extremely sensitive. As long as we were a small-time yard rag, we weren't a threat to "the ways things were." But the minute we achieved some renown, we made people nervous. Again, Jack's far-sighted philosophy went to work. He told us to continue the good work. I once overheard him ask one of his superiors if they would rather have us writing about our grievances or throwing rocks through windows as they did at other prisons. Jack fought for us, and I think that was when I really began to see that this man practiced what he preached to the men that lived at his prison.

It was about this time he came up with a ludicrous and far-fetched idea. He wanted to make the whole prison a drug-free environment! That wasn't nearly as unbelievable as the way he proposed it could happen. He suggested that we, the men who lived here, would be the deciding factor in the success of failure or this goal. Everyone, staff and prisoners alike, thought he was crazy. Prison is not a place for sticking your nose into anyone else's business, and Jack was insisting that everyone get involved.

At first I resisted. Even though by then I was an outspoken advocate of sobriety and would give my time freely to those who asked, I didn't see it as my job to tell some guy who didn't want to stop that he shouldn't get high anymore. I'd had people doing that to me ever since I'd started getting high, and I knew firsthand how futile those efforts had been with me. Not only that, they were dangerous.

Up until that point, Jack Cowley had gained much more than my respect. Without him, this prison wouldn't have had a substance abuse treatment program. Without him, this prison wouldn't have led the state in the number of outside volunteers who came inside and made such tremendous impacts on our lives. Without him, nine prisoners wouldn't have been certified in reality therapy and wouldn't have been doing counseling work with our peers. Without him, this would've been just another prison where people did their time and were warehoused until they got out. Without him, you wouldn't be reading this because this book never would've been written.

Still, like everyone else, I thought he'd lost his marbles, until I saw him in action outside of prison. The speak-out group I was involved in could travel. We were invited to area schools, churches, and other civic centers to share our experience, strength, and hope with others, especially youth. It was about that time that Jack made a couple of trips with us, and we shared the microphone.

We went to a church in Ardmore, Oklahoma, and I listened as Jack fielded questions. It was clear that, even in church, people were more concerned about punishment than they were forgiveness and reconciliation. I was impressed because he told them the same thing he'd been telling us—anyone could lock someone up, but the key to rehabilitation is grounded in love. He urged them to remember what Jesus said about how to treat those in prison.

The next stop was a parent-teacher conference in Noble. Here Jack told an auditorium full of people that unless they got actively involved in their own neighborhoods, and in their neighbors' lives, then we wouldn't be able to build enough prisons. He told them that the crime problem began in society and not in prison, and that simply building more prisons to battle crime was like backing ambulances up at the bottom of a cliff to pick up the people who fall as opposed to putting a fence at the edge of that cliff.

HBO did a special on our nations' prisons and filmed a large part of it right here in Oklahoma. Jack became my hero when he looked into the camera and told the nation that prisons—the way they were currently being operated—were set up to fail. He told people that if prisons ever became successful, they would ensure their own extinction. Corrections work was becoming too big an industry—too many people were basing their careers on our failures—for the system to let that happen.

After that, instead of a far-fetched dreamer, I saw a visionary, quite like an angry young Jesus overturning tables in a temple where the original purpose had been corrupted.

And, like Jesus, Jack was attacked. Fired. Officially, they called it a reassignment. In reality it was the first step toward putting him out to pasture.

I was mad. He was selling out, I believed. The department was transferring him to the Oklahoma State Reformatory, a hotbed of trouble. They were trying to paint the move as if it were being done so he could work his magic there. On the day he left, I asked him if that was really the case, and the look in his eyes, coupled with his silence, confirmed my belief.

Once at the reformatory, he began to make huge changes, trying to implement his philosophy at a place where they were truly still stuck in the Dark Ages. It was disastrous. Oklahoma State Reformatory was infamous for its protective custody units—places where men who had informed on other men were housed because they were afraid for their safety. Jack did away with that system and told people that they were going to have to be accountable for their own actions: you get in trouble, face the heat, don't tell on someone else, and expect him to protect you.

As he'd done at Harp, he opened the prison up and gave people chances to make right decisions. At Harp he hadn't begun his move until he had the full support of his staff. At Oklahoma State Reformatory, he didn't have the time for that luxury. Since the reformatory had been stuck so long in the dark ages, it was too big a jump for staff and prisoners and wrong decisions prevailed. The same philosophy that had worked magic at Harp and gave many a man his life back, ended in two murders and two escapes. Those events ended Jack's career and marked the end of a disappointing short-lived era. The house that Jack built was bulldozed away.

But Jack built something that can't be removed. He built people, and in this person, he built hope.

A guy can't have too many heroes.

# Forward Day by Day

*Saturday, March 10, 2001 — Ember Day*

✜

*The Samaritan woman said to him,*
*"How is it that you, a Jew, ask a drink of me, a woman of Samaria?"*
*(Jews do not share things in common with Samaritans.)*
— JOHN 4:9

If you've ever been anywhere in leg irons, belly chain, and handcuffs, you'll know. If you were black in the days of "whites only" signs or a minority victim of those same unwritten signs today, you'll know, or if you had to wear hand-me-downs to school, while everyone else wore Nikes, you'll know. If you were ever the only one in a long checkout line who had to pay for your food with food stamps, you'll know. If you've ever felt uncomfortable around someone else because you were different—and usually, that manifests itself as a feeling of less than—you'll know.

The story of Jesus and the Samaritan woman ends with Jesus talking about living waters and that's usually the focus or the moral of the story.

What about the social implication? How many barriers—concrete, steel, mental, emotional—do we erect every day? How many encounters—miraculous, monumental, life-changing—do we miss because of our barriers? How often do we miss out on giving and/or receiving the water of life?

Today, why don't you reenact the gospel and give someone you wouldn't ordinarily associate with a drink? The story continues, you know.

I Will: Strive for Justice

# Forward Day by Day

*Wednesday, March 21, 2001*

✠

*I judge no one.*
— JOHN 8:15B

You must be a tremendously open-minded person to even be willing to read my words. Who am I to touch these holy scriptures and offer my thoughts to people?

A copy of my book ended up on the desk of our governor and one of his staff. I didn't get to speak to the governor, but I did get to speak to the staff person.

"I was a prosecutor before I took this job," he began. "It was my job to lock people like you up. When I was given your book by a friend, I refused to read it. A murderer wasn't going to tell me anything."

Thankfully, he read it. Afterward he made it a point to come meet me. We actually became allies of a sort. The fact that we both liked each other was undeniable.

Ever since I began to follow this urging and attempt to use this gift, I've been amazed at the acceptance of people. Lots of them say that at first they were hesitant. After all....

It's beyond my understanding that you would not be reluctant to accept my interpretations on God, scripture, and life in general. I'm hesitant to offer them. I want you to know that. I'm not qualified to tell anyone anything. Who am I to write these meditations? No one, that's who. I've done the worst thing a person can do. Thank you for not holding that against me. You teach me about Jesus.

# Forward Day by Day

*Wednesday, May 8, 2002*

✛

*Your hands have made and fashioned me.*
— PSALM 119:73

"Man, all them guys are worthless." He spit it out. Actually, he was more specific and colorful in his statement.

We live next door to one another. We talk frequently. Both know the other is as far from sainthood as…well, you know. He's doing life without parole, and I'm doing life. Both have killed another man. On that basis alone we come crawling to God, never mind the million and one other shortcomings.

"Do you think it's possible for me to hate another group of people so much and still love God?" His frustration is still a tangible reality, partly because it took place less than twenty minutes ago and also because his feelings were trueborn.

"Well, brother," I was hesitant to step out there, "I know God made them, and I know God made us, so we're all good. I don't know exactly how I know that; it's just one of those things I know."

At the moment, I didn't know it was going to be today's meditation. Only when I read the above line from Psalm 119 did I know what to write about. Have you ever heard that saying—I don't remember exactly what it says at first, but it ends with "God don't make junk"? Well, God don't. Besides, if God does make junk, I qualify. Likewise, if God makes miracles, I qualify as well.

I Will: Strive for Justice

# Forward Day by Day

*Saturday, May 18, 2002*

✠

*Then suddenly a woman*
*who had been suffering from hemorrhages for twelve years*
*came up behind him and touched the fringe of his cloak.*
— MATTHEW 9:20

In the caste system of Jesus' day, this woman was as "untouchable" as they came. In that culture, it was all about being clean or unclean. One of the many reasons Jesus is my hero is that he stood against exclusive systems. The religious leaders—imperfect, clay-footed people themselves—decided who belonged, who was worthy, who could enter.

Even though Jesus taught us otherwise, we continually move contrary to the spirit of the gospel. We keep slapping Jesus in his face as we continually fail to get the point.

Words like, "heathens, pilgrims, savages, and slaves," litter our history, as do signs like, "We don't serve Indians," and water fountains with "White" and "Colored" over them.

Have we moved beyond? As the blinding light of our own self-proclaimed enlightenment shines in our eyes, let's not fail to see our cities are still segregated and we still judge people based on how similar they are to us. Religions still claim to be "the only way," white women still clutch their purses a little tighter when black men walk by, and homeless people are hard to look in the eye.

I, too, am as dirty as they come, and he let me touch his cloak.

# Forward Day by Day

*Monday, June 3, 2002*

⛾

*The wise have eyes in their head,*
*but fools walk in darkness.*
*Yet I perceived that the same fate befalls all of them.*
— ECCLESIASTES 2:14

Every morning, during summer months, a crew of fellow prisoners goes out to the ball field to cut the grass and keep up the grounds. This crew, even though dressed in the same faded blue state-issue clothes, stands apart from the rest of us. Their shirts have stains all over the front and haven't seen an iron in ages. Their haircuts are not as tidy, and their hair is usually dirty. Overall, their hygiene is considerably worse. These men are from the prison's mental health unit.

Most of the people I know look down on them. Had I not had the privilege of working on that unit some years ago, I would too. Granted, some of their behaviors are a bit out there, but they are people. And yet it's easy to look at them and think, "other."

I was running this morning and noticed a young man with wild blonde hair, pushing a mower. He'd push it a few feet, stop, walk in front of the mower, bend over and pick something up before resuming mowing. Then he'd repeat the process.

I thought, what a weirdo, until I saw that he was picking the flowers that sprinkled the grass. I guess he didn't want to butcher them with the mower. Then, instead of a weirdo I thought, "I might've seen Jesus."

The light. It shines on, I'm telling you.

I Will: Strive for Justice

# Forward Day by Day

## Saturday, June 22, 2002

✠

*What then? Are we any better off?*
*No, not at all; for we have already charged that all,*
*both Jews and Greeks, are under the power of sin.*
— ROMANS 3:9

Our prisons are full of men and women who have been told they were bad for as long as they can remember. The implication is alarming. You don't have to be in prison to know people who have been told all their life they'd never amount to anything, they were worthless, miserable, stupid, ugly, dirty.

What do they call it? Original sin? Why not just Born Bad? What good can come out of a belief in an inherent dirtiness? Don't get me wrong, I'm all for admitting our powerlessness and limitations, even our darkness. Believe me, I know that without God, I am nothing. I understand the thinking behind this doctrine, and I agree with the part of it that says we need God. We do. Badly.

However, there is another doctrine, not so widely circulated. Its Latin name is *Imago Dei*. It focuses on our being made in the image of God. What about that? We like to say, "I'm only human," as a means of excusing our mistakes. What if, instead, we picked ourselves up, dusted off the seat of our pants, and tried again? We could say, "I'll get this right; after all, I'm part divine."

Most of us already know how bad we are. We're in dire need of the knowledge of our goodness.

# Forward Day by Day

*Tuesday, July 9, 2002*

✠

*If anyone kills another, the murderer shall be put to death.*
— NUMBERS 35:30

Maybe you can say the above scripture real fast, and it'll seem less condemning. You may be able to relegate it to some category reserved for antiquated sayings, adages along the lines of "early to bed and early to rise."

However, I can tell you that from this side of the fence, standing in my footprints, you can't say it fast enough. No matter how it rolls off my tongue, it's a rock hurled straight at my head. I'd like to duck, believe me.

Fancying myself a wordsmith, I am aware of the ambiguities of words. For instance, "the kingdom is at hand," means, to literalists, that Jesus has left the building but will be returning from the clouds any minute now so everyone better be ready. If you're among those who tend to look a little beneath the surface, you may believe that it means with a simple opening of one's heart, one can find Jesus never left, he's standing right beside you, smack dab in the middle of the most incredible existence available to mortals.

The Numbers text needs no interpretation. Its candor makes me wince. Here I am pleading for my physical freedom. Right now, it seems I ought to be begging for my breath, my heartbeat, as opposed to a change of address.

Please, God.

---

I Will: Strive for Justice

# Forward Day by Day

*Wednesday, July 24, 2002*

✛

*Then they spat in his face and struck him;*
*and some slapped him, saying,*
*"Prophesy to us, you Messiah! Who is it that struck you?"*
— MATTHEW 26:67-68

He was as bloody as anyone I'd ever seen. His long hair was matted with the red, clumpy, sticky goo that ran from the gashes that showed white in his skull. He was sitting on a bench where his attackers had surrounded him, finally forcing him off his feet. He looked up through all that carnage and his eyes caught mine.

I didn't want to get involved. In prison, when the guards roll up on a scene like that, they'll round everyone up, and people who had nothing to do with the disturbance can spend days, even weeks, in lock-up. Not only did I not want to be involved in that respect, I didn't know the guy or the situation. Maybe he'd started it. Maybe…oh, bull, bottom line was I was scared to do what was right and step in and say, "Hey, don't y'all think he's had enough?"

I like to think I would've stood up for Jesus had I seen someone treating him like the passage from Matthew says they did. I would've rushed to his side and done like the president's Secret Service men, throwing my body between him and harm. I wouldn't let anyone beat up Jesus.

If they would have asked Jesus who it was that struck him, he would've pointed a bloody finger at me.

He would've been right.

---

# In Transition

*Wednesday, March 24, 2004*

⁜

*Jesus said to them, "I am the bread of life.*
*Whoever comes to me will never be hungry,*
*and whoever believes in me will never be thirsty."*
— JOHN 6:35

There are plenty of kids here in the United States who go to bed hungry more nights than not. Is it because they or their parents do not believe in Jesus? How about the millions of African children who die of hunger every day? Not enough Jesus in their lives?

Does this bit of scripture not suggest that? It sure seems to say that. Unless this walk with the One who made us, this relationship with the One who must have foreseen plenty of hunger, hurt, and even horrendous death, is about more than us getting what we want. Perhaps the beauty of this rebel movement that started in first-century Palestine—where oppression and injustice were more the rule than the exception—is that, regardless of our outside circumstances, or external factors, or our conditions, life can be good. It can be better than good. It can be so awesome that you might call it the kingdom.

There are plenty of growling bellies and parched throats that continue to hunger and thirst. Is it because every single one of them refuses to "come to Jesus"? Wouldn't that be a convenient explanation for those of us who do not go to bed hungry every night? After all, it is not our fault they do not believe.

People are going to go to bed hungry, people are going to die of hunger—as long as those of us who have food refuse to feed them.

This is true whether the hungry person is outside your door right now, digging through the dumpster at a restaurant tomorrow morning, or continents away.

This statement of Jesus is true on a spiritual level. The bread he offers is of another world and transcends physical hunger and thirst.

Likewise, the bread and water we have in our cabinets can also help ease people's hunger and thirst. When we do, some of that bread and water Jesus was talking about seems to get mixed in with it.

# People

*Praying Day by Day, 2009*

✠

*Treat all men alike.*
*Give them all the same laws.*
*Give them all an even chance to live and grow.*
*All men were made by the same Great Spirit Chief.*
*They are all brothers.*
*The earth is the mother of all people,*
*and all people should have equal rights upon it.*
—Hin-mah-too-yah-lat-kekt (Chief Joseph),
Nez Perce Leader (1840-1909)

Oral history tells of a time when Cochise began to see the end of the Apaches' fight with the settlers and the United States Army. He was so convinced the end was near that he sought out the chief blue coat, and they talked of peace.

Cochise told the general his people were ragged and starving from running, and he just wanted to find a place for them to live in peace. He pointed out his people had once lived in the Cañada Alamosam and he wondered if they could live there again. It is said that the general told him there were three hundred Mexicans living there, brand-new American citizens and landowners, and they couldn't make them move.

Cochise reportedly saw no problem with this and told the general so. There was plenty of room, he said. Just put us farther down from them, make us citizens and landowners too, and we will take on your ways.

The general shook his head. "No, we can't do that."

Cochise wanted to know why.

I Will: Strive for Justice

"Because you can't become citizens and own land."

Why?

"Indians are not people. It is the law."

As we seek to walk in the sunlight and see the Master's thumbprint on all peoples, it will help to be honest about our history; how we came to be here now and also how others arrived where they are. Only then can we move on.

# Defining Fences

*Praying Day by Day, 2009*

✠

*Are not two sparrows sold for a penny?*
*Yet not one of them will fall to the ground apart from your Father.*
— MATTHEW 10:29

The sparrow hopped over a concrete barrier that divided a ten-foot-wide graveled area from a well-manicured lawn. A twelve-foot-tall chain link fence topped with sharp razor wire marked the other side of the graveled area and divided it from another well-manicured lawn.

The sparrow hopped around for a minute, through the fence, and back into the graveled area. It hopped some more, traveling through rolls of coiled concertina wire, seemingly oblivious to the fact it was heading into a prison. Finally, it crossed the space between the fences and hopped back into the prison visiting area where I was sitting with my wife.

"Look," I said. A few hops down around our feet, in and around the picnic table, then back through the fence and graveled area, and the outside fence until it was hopping around in the "free world."

The sparrow didn't seem to recognize the implications of the fence. It seemed as content to hop inside the fence as it did outside the fence. In fact, it was clear that the essence of its being—its sparrowness, if you will—was not defined by which side of the fence it hopped on.

Then I noticed that the sun shined on the bird on both sides of the fence; the wind ruffled its little brown, gray, and black feathers on both sides. And, the little sparrow sang on both sides, too. The fence wasn't a defining force in the sparrow's life and that day it became less of one in mine.

What fences define you?

I Will: Strive for Justice

# Forward Day by Day

*Saturday, April 9, 2011*

✛

*When many of his disciples heard it, they said,*
*"This teaching is difficult; who can accept it?"*
— JOHN 6:60

I know people in recovery from alcoholism and other addictions who will answer their phone in the middle of the night, drive hundreds of miles to help someone, and show up for meetings week after week to set up chairs and make coffee and listen and nod. When someone says that behavior is noble or worthy or impressive, the recovering person replies that the only reason he does it is because he's already tried every other available route.

Some of these folks will even go so far as to tell you they still occasionally stray to that easier, softer path, looking to coast down life's highway. But they are inevitably reminded that their path remains the same. Much like the author of today's gospel reading reports, recovery is a "difficult teaching," and the main reason people adhere to it is because it is their last available choice.

A man tells a story of bringing the book *Alcoholics Anonymous* home to his mom, who wanted to read it, seeing how it had helped her son. Her report was this: "I found it simple and redundant." Difficult teachings usually are.

# Forward Day by Day

*Tuesday, April 12, 2011*

✠

*His parents said this because they were afraid of the Jews.*
— JOHN 9:22A

Nobody wants to stand up against the way things are. Jesus did, of course, which is one of the reasons we're still talking about him. But it was also his irreverence for the established order that got him killed.

Where I work, there are some who rule supreme. Words come out of their mouths indisputable and, once they've said something, it just is. When I first questioned this, I was told they'd always done it this way.

I was leaving the building and heard my name. It was a patient, a young lady visiting with her family. She was in tears. She'd been told her family could bring pictures of her baby, but now they were told it wasn't allowed. Would I, she wondered, be willing to go back and ask on her behalf?

I did and was told no with a look that said I was outside my scope. I relayed the message. The woman and her family looked up at me, and all I saw was defeat. "Where are the pictures?" I asked. I retrieved them and then stood and watched as they looked through them. I think I got it right.

I Will: Strive for Justice

# Forward Day by Day

*Saturday, April 16, 2011*

✠

*No longer shall they teach one another, or say to each other,*
*"Know the LORD," for they shall all know me.*
— JEREMIAH 31:34

Long ago in what is now Oklahoma, the Kiowa people and the buffalo had a sacred relationship. Though the U.S. government had told the Kiowas they would be allowed to live there, the buffalo knew better. Soon, treaties were broken and railroads appeared. Buffalo were slaughtered; only thirty remained out of more than a million. Mountains of sun-bleached buffalo bones littered the landscape. The leader of the buffalo, sensing the inevitable, took the remaining herd and they vanished into Mount Scott, a sacred place near present day Lawton.

That morning, a young Kiowa woman was out walking in the mist when she saw the last of the buffalo walking toward Mount Scott. The mountain opened and in walked the buffalo. It is no coincidence that at about the same time, the Kiowa people who wouldn't agree to relocate were rounded up and imprisoned—where many died from starvation and exposure.

Jeremiah, like many Old Testament books, tells a story of a people coming to know their God. As we seek to live together in this world, it is wise to understand there are many different peoples—and they, too, have their stories.

# God Is...

*Seeking God Day by Day, 2013*

✛

*The pig is taught by sermons and epistles*
*to think the God of Swine has snout and bristles.*
— AMBROSE BIERCE,
FROM THE DEVIL'S DICTIONARY

It comforts me to know that a hundred years ago there was someone else wondering if framing God in strictly human terms was the only way to paint a picture of the Alpha and the Omega, the Almighty, the Creator of All that is and ever will be.

There is a God; I don't struggle with that. I do, however, struggle with all of our attempts to comprehend and explain the incomprehensible and the unexplainable.

Thousands of years ago the ancient Greek poet and philosopher Xenophanes wrote, "If oxen and horses and lions had hands and were able to draw with their hands and do the same things as men, horses would draw the shapes of gods to look like horses and oxen would draw them to look like oxen, and each would make the gods' bodies have the same shape as they themselves had."

As far back as we know, almost every world religion has claimed to be the way. Don't get me wrong. I get it; the best I can do is understand something through what I can see, touch, feel, smell, taste, think. I shouldn't expect more from anyone else.

However, anthropomorphism—seeing nonhuman things in human form—can be dangerous, as author Anne Lamott quips when she points out that you can safely assume you've created God in your own image when it turns out that God hates all the same people you do.

# Forward Day by Day

*Wednesday, February 5, 2014*

⁜

*When they came to the place that God had shown him,*
*Abraham built an altar there and laid the wood in order.*
*He bound his son Isaac and laid him on the altar,*
*on top of the wood.*
*Then Abraham reached out his hand*
*and took the knife to kill his son.*
— GENESIS 22:9-10

Today, if someone says the Lord told them to kill their offspring, they're judged to be mentally ill and are locked up in a mental institution. Yet, we still use this story of Abraham and Isaac to illustrate faith. I like it for another parallel: what are we willing to give up so we can get what we want?

Many people are in debt and say they want out. Are they willing to cut up their credit cards, quit eating out and driving new cars, and live within their means?

People with addictions say they want to stop getting in trouble and disappointing themselves and those around them. Are they willing to give up that immediate feel-good fix for a solution that takes some time and work but results in a delayed, but much richer, gratification?

People want to lose weight, live healthier, and feel better but won't exercise or change diets.

Sacrifice means something different for everyone. What comes to your mind?

# Forward Day by Day

*Monday, February 17, 2014*

✠

*Yours are the heavens; the earth also is yours;*
*you laid the foundations of the world and all that is in it.*
— PSALM 89:11

In the 1930s, it became known as "No Man's Land"—the Oklahoma Panhandle, the western third of Kansas, southeastern Colorado, the northern two-thirds of the Texas Panhandle, and northeastern New Mexico. Due to drought and short-sighted, ill-advised farming practices, Mother Nature and man clashed—and Mother Nature won.

This all began with plowing up the native grasslands of the Great Plains to plant wheat for great profit. When wheat prices plummeted, people plowed and planted more in an attempt to recoup their losses. Drought, a naturally occurring cyclical event, came next. Soon, the winds of the Great Plains blew the dirt away, eventually all the way to Washington, D. C., and New York City.

Some of the original reactions were to pave the area or cover it in chicken wire. (You can't make this stuff up.) Eventually, the government purchased four million acres and returned it to native grassland.

There are many ways we can fail to recognize God in creation; the Dust Bowl was a natural and man-made disaster of biblical proportions. That was less than a hundred years ago.

I Will: Strive for Justice

# Forward Day by Day

*Thursday, February 27, 2014*

✠

*Store up my commandments with you…*
*that they may keep you from the loose woman,*
*from the adulteress with her smooth words.*
— PROVERBS 7:1, 5

Beginning with Eve, women have been viewed in a less than honorable light in the Bible. They're often painted as temptresses, and godly women are expected to have a subservient nature. Speaking of subservient, slavery is also condoned in our Holy Book, going as far as instructions on how to treat slaves. Likewise, there are sacrifices, executions, and stonings.

Some people take every word in the Bible literally. Others say we have to understand what's literal and what's metaphorical. Some look at the historical context, saying that what was written reflects the culture of the times—the author's attempt to explain the unexplainable. Some go as far as to say that if the Bible was written by racist and sexist men, they don't need it as a moral compass and wonder about the God it claims to represent. Yet others have their own holy book, full of its own contradictions and inspiration.

As I walk through all these camps, my hope is that I treat everyone with dignity, kindness, and respect—and let the light that has saved me from myself show in my actions.

# About the Author

Bo Cox has written inspirational and down-to-earth meditations for Forward Movement for nearly twenty years. His first set of reflections were published in *Forward Day by Day* in 1995, when he was still serving a life sentence for first-degree murder. His stories of struggle, his honesty, and his uncanny insights immediately resonated with readers, making him one of Forward Movement's most popular writers.

Bo has written for nine months of *Forward Day by Day*, meditations for Lent, a collection of essays for *God Is Not In the Thesaurus: Stories from an Oklahoma Prison*, and as a contributor to other books.

Released from prison in 2003, Bo and his wife—and dogs and cats—enjoy their home near Norman, Oklahoma—a sanctuary nestled in the woods. Bo leads therapeutic activities at a psychiatric hospital. He also serves as a consultant to St. Albans School in Washington, D.C.